# REFLECTIVE PRACTICE AND PERSONAL DEVELOPMENT

## in Counselling & Psychotherapy

SECOND EDITION

# REFLECTIVE PRACTICE AND PERSONAL DEVELOPMENT

## in Counselling & Psychotherapy

## SOFIE BAGER-CHARLESON

**⑤SAGE**

Los Angeles | London | New Delhi
Singapore | Washington DC | Melbourne

**$\bigcirc$ SAGE**

Los Angeles | London | New Delhi
Singapore | Washington DC | Melbourne

SAGE Publications Ltd
1 Oliver's Yard
55 City Road
London EC1Y 1SP

SAGE Publications Inc.
2455 Teller Road
Thousand Oaks, California 91320

SAGE Publications India Pvt Ltd
B 1/I 1 Mohan Cooperative Industrial Area
Mathura Road
New Delhi 110 044

SAGE Publications Asia-Pacific Pte Ltd
3 Church Street
#10-04 Samsung Hub
Singapore 049483

Editor: Susannah Trefgarne
Assistant editor: Ruth Lilly
Production editor: Rachel Burrows
Marketing manager: Dilhara Attygalle
Cover design: Naomi Robinson
Typeset by: C&M Digitals (P) Ltd, Chennai, India

This book was first published in 2010 as *Reflective Practice in Counselling and Psychotherapy* under the Learning Matters imprint. Reprinted 2016 (twice), 2017 (twice), 2018 (twice), 2019 (twice)
This second edition published 2020

**Library of Congress Control Number: 2020931238**

**British Library Cataloguing in Publication data**

A catalogue record for this book is available from the British Library

ISBN 978-1-5264-7750-7
ISBN 978-1-5264-7749-1 (pbk)

# Contents

# About the author and contributors

**Sofie Bager-Charleson** is a UKCP and BACP registered psychotherapist and supervisor. She works at the Metanoia Institute as Director of Studies on the MPhil/PhD in Psychotherapy. She chairs the research group Therapist as a Research Practitioner (TRP) focusing on obstacles and opportunities for psychotherapists and counselling psychologists to develop into confident research practitioners. She is also the instigator and co-founder of the annual Metanoia Research Academy for practitioners. Sofie has published widely in the field of practitioner research and reflexivity in peer-reviewed articles, book chapters, guest editorials and textbooks like *Practice-based Research in Therapy: A Reflexive Approach* (SAGE, 2014) and *Enjoying Research in the Field of Therapy* (Palgrave MacMillan 2020, in press).

**Simon du Plock** is Faculty Head for Post-Qualification and Professional Doctorates at the Metanoia Institute, London, UK where he directs counselling psychology and psychotherapy research doctorates. He is also a Chartered Counselling Psychologist, and a Founding Member of the BPS Register of Psychologists Specialising in Psychotherapy. He lectures internationally on aspects of existential therapy and has authored over eighty book chapters and papers in peer-reviewed academic journals.

**Biljana van Rijn** heads the Faculty for Research Strategy and Innovation at Metanoia Institute, where she has established a long-standing research clinic with an emphasis on routine outcomes evaluation of humanistic and integrative psychotherapies.

Her publications focus on clinical assessment and formulation, and an emphasis on reflective, relational practice. She works as a psychotherapist and supervisor in Surrey and has authored a range of research papers and other publications.

**Jeannie Wright** is Visiting Professor at the University of Malta. She has been involved in counsellor education for over thirty years and has been writing what she couldn't say for more years than that. She has developed practice-based research in counselling and writing for therapeutic purposes in seven different universities in the UK, Europe, the South Pacific and most recently at the University of Malta.

# 1

# Reflective practice: An overview

## Core knowledge

Some of the key terms guiding this chapter are:

- Different models for reflection and reflective practice.
- 'Reflection in' and 'reflection on' practice, as distinguished by Donald Schön. This includes considering 'on-the-spot experiments' as well as systematic retrospective learning.
- The concepts of espoused theory and theory-in-use, as introduced by Schön and Argyris to explore the interesting gap between what professionals say they do and how they actually practice.
- Double-loop learning, which aims to highlight underlying values and assumptions in decision making at work.
- The TSS-ACCTT 'map' aims to support you in 'looping back' on critical decisions. TSS stands for **T**heory, **S**elf and **S**ocio-culture as filters or lenses to loop back through when considering difficult decisions and problems. ACCTT reflects phases from **A**cknowledging (sensing, feeling, noticing) a problem, to **C**onnecting and **C**onsidering it in context of your self, your theory and socio-cultural framing for practice, before **T**ransforming practice and sometimes developing therapeutic **T**heory with your new learning.

## Reflective practice

Reflective practice rests on a critical appreciation of theory, self and the socio-cultural context for our practice. It involves 'looping back' on events in our practice from different angles guided by an openness for continuous transformative learning. It has been documented, critiqued and developed across different disciplines. In this chapter, both forerunners' and later thinkers' theories on reflective practice will be explored, starting with Kant's still relevant definition of 'reflection':

> Reflection is not concerned with objects themselves, in order to obtain concepts from them directly, but is a state of the mind in which we first set ourselves to discover the subjective conditions under which we can arrive at concepts. (Kant, 1781/2007: 264)

We will explore some of the critiques about reflective practice as 'too broad' versus 'too descriptive'. We will return to some key principles suggested by Donald Schön who coined the phrase 'reflective practice'. Reflective practice will be explored with the therapists' needs and interests at heart. The personal development angle to reflective practice involves listening to, considering and exploring what you might need to thrive and develop as part of your relational practice.

## Both simple and complex

Simply put, reflective practice is about how we make our decisions in practice. The complexity becomes obvious when we think of explaining 'actions' in movement-related practices, like skiing, driving a car or acting as a stuntman. Most actions rely on learnt, internalised and intuitive knowledge to progress; stopping to explain and consider what *exactly* might be going on – for instance in scientific terms – is neither helpful nor an option. Some practices offer more time to reflect in action than others: psychotherapy offers a particularly well-suited practice for reflecting-in-action. The underpinning interest for reflective practice revolves, in short, around the mystery of 'thinking on ones' feet', e.g., how to without much thinking time respond to events decisively and effectively. Approaching the process 'the other way around' can sometimes help to highlight the complexities involved in this: starting with *not* acting can be helpful to explore how learnt, internalised as well as intuitive responses come into play. The following exercise is intended to help to support you explore the space between your experiences of something within a therapeutic relationship, and informed or automatic responses.

---

### Activity 1.1 Hearing the other

You need a partner for this exercise, which revolves around listening without any interruption. You will each take turns to talk about a topic of your own choice for five minutes, without any interruptions by the other at all.

Checklist:

- Have you got a watch?
- Have you agreed on what to do if any unforeseen strong emotions should arise?

**Activity:** Talk about a chosen, personal subject for five minutes. The listener will remain silent, listening without any interruptions at all.
Afterwards, for the listener:

- How did *not* intervening make you feel? When – if at all – did remaining silent seem like an issue? What might you have wanted to put forward, at what point?
- Concentrate on connecting with all your responses during your listening – what happened inside you when listening?
- How can your response be understood in context of your *personal background*?
- How – if at all – does your *modality* help to understand your responses?

**Activity**: Take turns.
Discuss and share experiences around your learnt, internalised responses versus spontaneous, perhaps surprising reactions during this 'session'. Did you have time to consider the difference between the two?

## The 'TSS-ACCTT' map

The conundrum of moving from an experience to some form of knowledge – ideally guided by informed decisions made whilst *in* action – is, as suggested, both simple and complex. What Schön (1983) famously describes as the 'swampy lowlands of practice', has been explored from multiple perspectives. The aim of the 'TSS-ACCTT' map (Figure 1.1) below is to support your thinking around your own reflective practice. TSS stands for **T**heory, **S**elf and **S**ocio-culture as contexts, or 'filters' for your reflections. ACCTT stands for **A**cknowledging, **C**onnecting, **C**onsidering and **T**ransforming practice as different phases of reflective practice.The TSS-ACCTT map integrates different approaches to reflective learning as conceptualised by, for instance, Schön (1983), Kolb (1984), Gibbs (1988, 2013), Johns (1995), Mezirow (2009) and Taylor (2006) in their models for experiential and transformative learning. Acknowledging, connecting and transforming represent, as suggested, 'phases' which move from simply noticing, sensing, feeling to connecting with a problem and critically considering it in context of your modality, with the view of informing and transforming your own – and sometimes others' – practice through your new learning. Personal development plays a key role in this process, your support and ongoing learning will be paramount. We will consider learning in context of different types of knowing, including sensing, feeling (aesthetic) and empirical knowing.

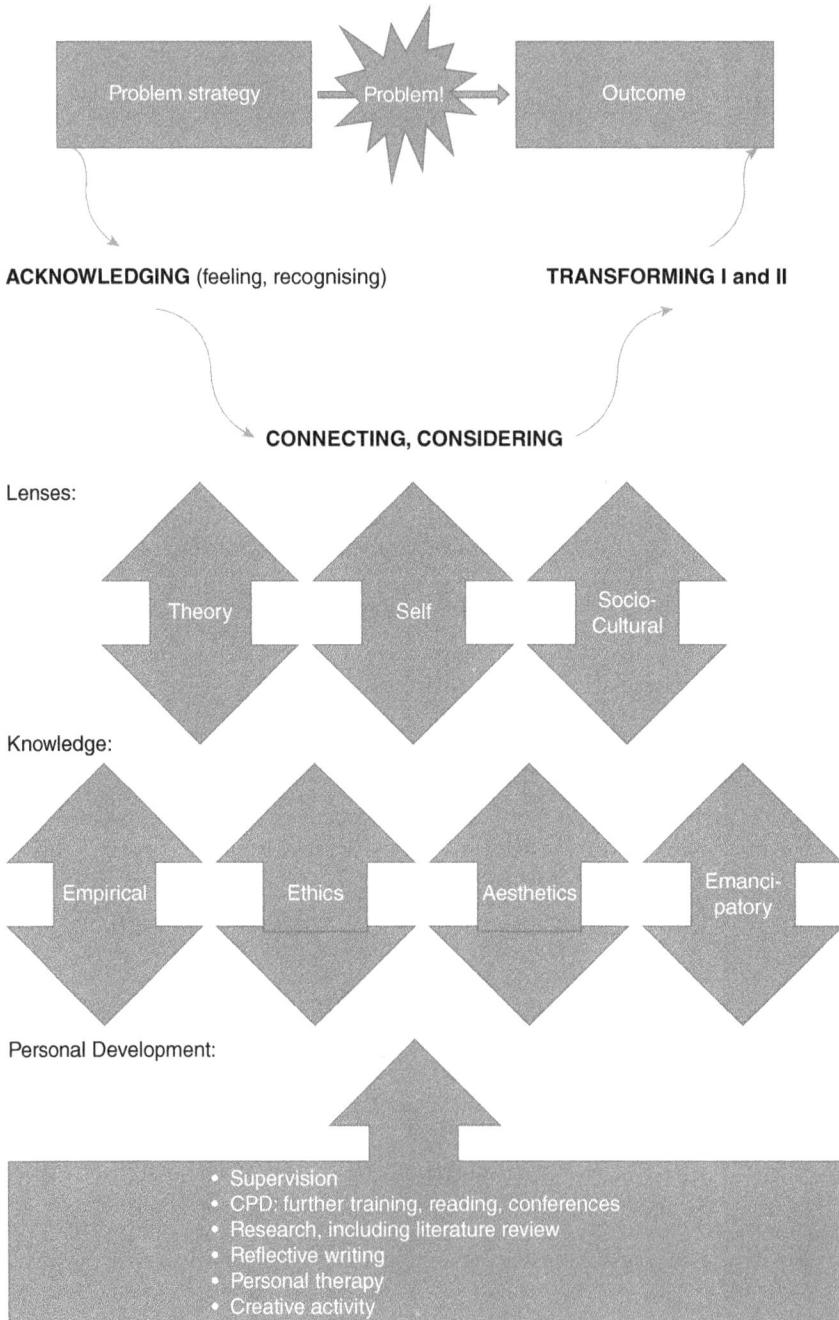

*Figure 1.1* TSS-ACCTT Model

## Reflective practice across different disciplines and time

The significance of reflective practice is well-documented across different disciplines. A simple literature review shows widespread references in, for instance

- education (Gibbs, 2013; Jay & Johnson, 2002; Rogers, 2001)
- social work (Ixer, 2016; White, Fook, & Gardner, 2008)
- nursing (Goulet, Larue, & Alderson, 2016; Johns, 1995)
- general psychology (Binks, Jones, Fergal, & Knight, 2013; Lewis, Virden, Hutchings, Smith, & Bhargava, 2011)
- applied sport psychology (Anderson, Knowles, & Gilbourne, 2004), including areas like sports coaching with studies titled: '[a]nother bad day at the training ground: coping with ambiguity in the coaching context' (Jones & Wallace, 2005: 121).

Ambiguity is a common theme in the studies relating to reflective practice, as is the prospect of 'learning from critical experiences'. The studies tend to refer to forerunners of reflective practice like Schön (1983), Kolb (1984) and Gibbs (1988) in particular.

## Forerunners

Kolb referred to learning as 'the process whereby knowledge is created through the transformation of experience' (Kolb, 1984: 41). Kolb's theory presents a cyclical model (Figure 1.2) of learning over of four stages.

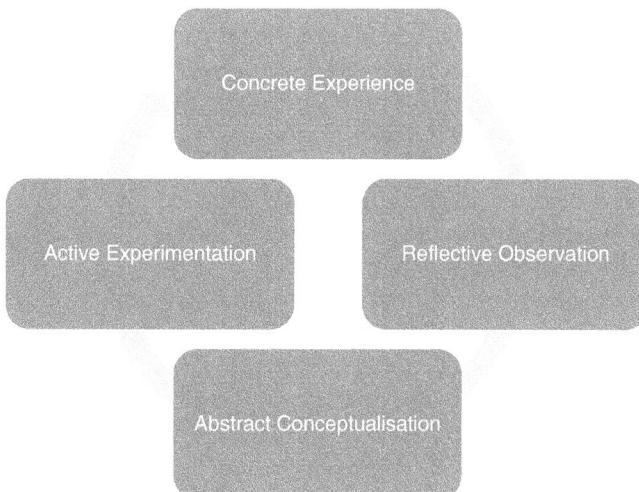

*Figure 1.2*   Kolb's transformation of experience as the basis for knowledge

The learner actively experiences an activity, then consciously reflects back on that experience, followed by making sense of it and experimenting with new solutions.

Gibbs (1988, 2013) added a significant emotional dimension to the reflective practice as highlighted in (Figure 1.3).

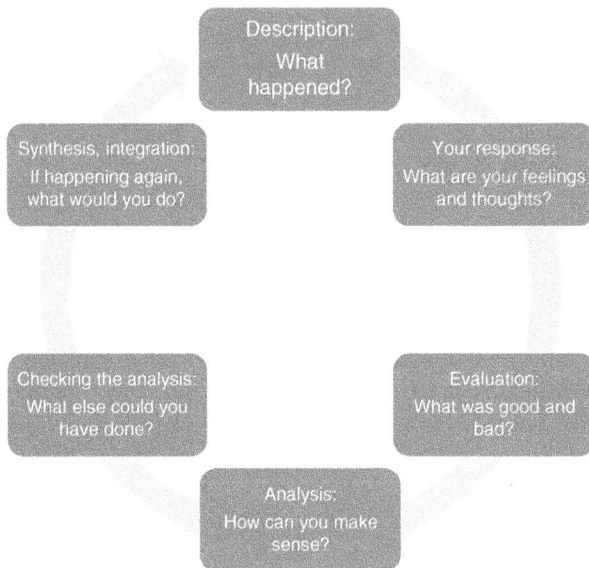

*Figure 1.3* Putting emotions into reflection, as adapted from Gibbs (1988, 2013)

## New models

The number of suggested models for reflective practice seems to be growing (Black & Plowright, 2010; Goulet, Larue, & Alderson, 2016; Nguyen, Fernandez, Karsenti, & Charlin, 2014). Based on a systematic literature review, Ruth-Sahd identifies outcomes of the reflective process:

- **Integration** of theoretical concepts to practice
- Increased **learning from experience**
- Enhanced **self-esteem** through learning
- Acceptance of professional responsibility and continual professional growth
- Enhanced **critical thinking** and judgement making in complex and uncertain situations, based on experience and prior knowledge, thereby enhancing patient care
- **Empowerment** of practitioners
- Increased social and political **emancipation**
- Improvement in practice by promoting **greater self-awareness**. (Ruth-Sahd, 2003: 490)

Ruth-Sahd synthesises a broad definition to cover the many references, with reflective practice as 'an imaginative, creative, nonlinear, human act in which educators and students recapture their experience, think about it, and evaluate it' (Ruth-Sahd, 2003: 450).

Ruth-Sahd criticises at the same time this broad and often blurred consensus of meaning, suggesting that 'authors and researchers define reflective practice by using their own lenses, worldviews, and experiences'. This broad definition mystifies and 'blurs a consensus of meaning'. Practitioners are 'being encouraged to ... promote reflective practice [but] shown very little evidence that it actually improves practice or results in learning' (Ruth-Sahd, 2003: 490).

Reflective practice is likely to disappoint if we seek a neat and tidy structure for it. Another, more recent systematic literature review is offered by Marshall (2019). His overview of literature across different professions resulted in the suggestion of four overarching themes within reflective practice, namely as a cognitive, integrative, iterative and active process.

- **Cognitive**. Used to make sense of complex and ambiguous problems. reflective practitioners are 'theoreticians of practice' (Marshall 2019: 399). Marshall refers, for instance, to Schön (1983) and Kolb (2014) who suggest searching for tentative, explanatory hypotheses which can be 'tested' through subsequent experiences and reflections.
- **Integrative**. Reflective practice involves analysing and synthesising different ideas and perspectives to integrate new experience with existing knowledge. This includes using reflective practice as a means of exploring one's own meaning-making processes including theory, emotions, values and beliefs to integrate new perspectives with the already known.
- **Iterative**. Reflective practice is an ongoing cyclic process with frequent returns (looping back) to one's interpretation of experiences and ideas.
- **Active**. Reflective practice includes active involvement based on deliberate, conscious attempts to make sense of an experience or idea and to integrate, or implement, this learning into new practice.

## Systematic questioning focusing different perspectives

Reflective practice always involves systematic questioning, but with different types of knowledge to the forefront. Beverley Taylor asserts that 'it simplifies the enormous task of thinking about reflection' if we think in terms of 'three main types of reflection' (Taylor, 2006: 15). Each type of reflection can be used alone or in combination with the others.

- **Technical reflection** is based on the scientific method and rational, deductive thinking, and will allow you to generate validated empirical knowledge through rigorous means so that you can be assured that work procedures are based on scientific reasoning.

- **Practical reflection** provides a systematic questioning process that encourages you to reflect deeply on role relationships, to locate their dynamics and habitual issues.
- **Emancipatory reflection** seeks to free you from taken-for-granted assumptions and oppressive forces that limit you and your practice.

## Affect – a neglected source of knowledge

Gibbs (1988) is, as mentioned, another of the forerunners in reflective practice. His Reflective Cycle starts with description, and continues clockwise to feelings, evaluation, analysis, conclusion and ends at action plan before returning to description. Gibbs stresses the importance of affect in reflective practice. He sees a danger in making reflective practice into a tick box exercise. He refers to integrating psychotherapeutic theory in teaching training, as part of reflective practice:

> As a young and enthusiastic teaching development professional, I spent my evenings and weekends trying to 'learn my trade' by attending Tavistock groups (Freudian), encounter groups (Rogerian), human relations workshops, co-counselling training, Interpersonal Process Recall, experiential methods workshops – it was a long list [of theory about] looking inside oneself, paying attention to the affect, and reflection.

> Reflective practice in teaching is illustrated here by a transdisciplinary integration based on reflection of self and new theory, which transforms into a focus 'not just on individual teachers, but on teachers paying attention to themselves and to their interpersonal relations with others ...'. (Gibbs, 2013: 12)

Gibbs worries, however, about the future. He concludes that:

> If one were to examine the sessions at annual [teaching] conferences today, this focus of attention is largely missing. We seem to have moved on to an affect-free world in which rationality prevails, driven by educational theory or by empirical evidence. (Gibbs, 2013: 14)

There are fortunately many good examples of transdisciplinary, integrative approaches to self-awareness, interaction and theory which serve as inspiring examples of rigorous reflective practice. The case study below is provided by Ozden Bademcia. It is about a recent teaching project with street children in Istanbul, Turkey, where school dropout, absenteeism, broken relationships and disruptive behaviour were identified as experienced problems. The regular educational strategies involved a discipline and/or reward system which upon evaluation needed improvement. The educational team decided to explore the childrens' behaviour in the context of attachment theory. One key member of the team studied psychosocial theory at Tavistock, London and helped, on her return, to implement an attachment-informed psychosocial programme in a school setting located in a poor neighbourhood. They devised a psychosocial programme where 40 university student mentors and their professors provided weekly psychosocial support to 160 year-one and year-two primary school-children over a period of eight months.

## Case Study 1.1

### Psychosocial theory in educational practice

Teachers' perceptions of an attachment-informed psychosocial programme for schoolchildren with social and emotional problems in Istanbul, Turkey:

Our objective was to create a secure proximity zone from which the university students acted the older and more knowledgeable secondary caregivers to the schoolchildren. During the programme, we used psychosocial activities such as library visits, reading and writing games, maths games, drawing, animations, calendar making and parachuting games (among others) to facilitate a secure learning environment in which children develop essential social skills and emotional maturity that helps them to navigate various stressful circumstances from childhood to adult life. We provided an attachment space within which children learned from older and more knowledgeable figures (student mentors and professors) on how to modulate disruptive behavior and anxieties. Compared with previous experiences, less emotional problems and less disruptive behaviours were reported (by the teacher we interviewed) whilst connectedness and empathic attachment relationships increased. (Bademcia et al., 2019)

Johns' (1995) model for reflective learning adds an emphasis on 'aesthetics' which also is captured in the ACCTT map, with the emphasis on sensing, feeling and engaging in problem on an initially intuitive level. The term sesthetic awareness is helpful to consider the significance of being moved or touched by an experience. Johns (1995) stressed the importance of including this to the repertoire of important kinds of knowledge and he listed them as

- Ethics – moral knowledge
- Personal – self awareness
- Aesthetics – knowledge approached through the felt senses and imagination rather than as already thinkable or material.

## Activity 1.2

Aesthesis means, in Greek, to perceive throughout the senses. How might the sensing, visceral and embodied side of knowledge impact your role as a therapist? Return to your responses in Activity 1.1, and consider how you related to and made sense of the listening 'session' with the knowledge types suggested by Johns above in mind.

The case study below captures the therapist Nicola Blunden's interest in understanding the sensing, feeling and embodied aspects of our practice more through research comparing the practice of therapists and musicians.

## Case Study 1.2

Nicola Blunden works as a senior lecturer in counselling and psychotherapy studies. She notices a change in their curriculum, where manualisation has taken precedence at – what seems to Nicola – the expense of therapists 'seeking to be present [aiming for] shared experience'. Nicola decides to turn to artists to learn more about practice as 'dialogical co-construction of personal narrative, idiographic and phenomenological in nature'. She is turning to the practice of artists, musicians, in particular, to learn more about 'aesthetic knowing'. Nicola writes:

'The psychotherapy profession is undergoing a crisis in identity. Broad tensions exist in its construction of itself either as a clinical and technological activity on the one hand, grounded in empirical evidence, and available for generalisation across medical populations; and on the other hand as a dialogical co-construction of personal narrative, idiographic and phenomenological in nature [...] This study will explore a third potential description of therapy as an aesthetic event ... As Kant proposed, aesthetic judgements comprise in-the-moment choices ... emerging from a "free play of imagination and understanding" ... Artists unite skill and form with here-and-now attunement, generating unique, ephemeral artefacts that nevertheless communicate universality. In art, then, the tensions between knowledge (skill and technology) and presence (spacious not-knowing) are embraced in the moment, in beautiful and creative ways. To a great extent, this practice echoes that of the psychotherapist and her client. In therapeutic dialogue, both parties pay attention to the tone, rhythm, meaning, and response of their words as well as their somatic and physical expressions. When both parties feel free from extrinsic concerns, the resulting experience and dialogue can feel sublime, profound and awesome. Similarly, dialogue can be conceived more as a duet than a debate, more as a dance than a symposium. This study seeks to survey the shared terrain between art and psychotherapy, as well as the borders and differences between them. Are therapists, like artists, seeking to be present, to make judgements of taste (why this word, with this tone, and at this moment), and to seek a shared experience of beauty or expression? If so, what does this mean for our clinical practice and for our methods.'

Johns writes about 'aesthetic knowing' as revolving around 'a perceptual, intuitive grasp of the whole situation, which can never be reduced to sets of rules to be technically applied to the situation' (Johns, 1995: 228). He distinguishes between 'empiric knowing' which encourages the practitioner 'to be dispassionate or detached, objective, rational' versus aesthetic knowing or response which *'always is influenced by the person of the practitioner and the degree to which, in the human encounter with the patient, the practitioner is prepared to be engaged'* (Johns, 1995: 228; emphasis added). The concept 'aesthetic diagnosis' (Roubal, Francesetti, & Gecele, 2017) is, for instance, referred to in Gestalt therapy for a 'contact process' where the therapists perceive and resonate with their client's suffering through his/her senses, and where the 'suffering' is a phenomenon that is co-created by the client and the therapist to be 'transformed' in the process of contact. Gestalt therapists attend to both what is figural and at the forefront for the client at different moments, and to what is in the (back) ground of the client's experience. Another example of a practitioner who dialectically considers her practice through transdisciplinary lenses is illustrated below by Helena Kallner turning to dance and movement to deepen our understanding about the shared and often unspoken 'resonance' in therapy.

## Case Study 1.3

### 'Psychotherapists use of movement and kinesthetic resonance in psychotherapy', by Helena Kallner

Helena incorporates movement, aesthetics and kinesthetic learning in her practice and training. She is interested in practitioners' experiences of using this in their practice. She draws from 'practical knowledge' in her research; a relatively new research approach which aims to avoid split between thinking and action which we will explore more later on. Helena writes:

'My research question about kinaesthetic resonance in psychotherapy has emerged from my personal and professional journey in gestalt psychotherapy. Movement has always been an important part of my life. What initially attracted me to gestalt therapy was the relational and experiential approach that allowed for and encouraged curiosity in embodiment and what Merleau-Ponty calls the lived body – what is felt and sensed in relation. However, in the beginning of my gestalt psychotherapy training I was surprised to find that body process was not attended to as much as I was expecting. The verbal dialogue was prioritized, and that confused me. I was struggling to translate my felt experience into the spoken language, as if I did not have a vocabulary that was close enough to what I sensed. I began to search for more experiential and embodied approaches to gestalt therapy, and that led me to study Developmental Somatic Psychotherapy, created by Ruella Frank, who explores how "experience" with an interest in how the body is touching, and simultaneously is being touched by "the world". This "reverberating responses" between us approached as "kinesthetic resonance" and refers to our sensed and aesthetic experience of a situation as lived by us in the moment. Finding a methodology congruent with my research topic has been an important journey for me. Research methodology provides a framework for my study. It is also "attitude" which will impact how I meet and engage with the research participants, and them with me. Phenomenology, and specifically the methods Finley describe as reflexive–relational approach, inspires me to transparently attend to and involve the relational dynamics between the researcher and the research participants. Studies in practical knowledge is a fast growing research tradition in Scandinavia, first developed by "Senter for praktisk kunskap" at the University

*(Continued)*

of Nordland in Norway. **Practical knowledge** is an interdisciplinary research area that approaches practical knowledge of skilled professionals – particularly those in which the ability to meet and relate to people are a core professional competence (teachers, nurses, police, etc.), often different from what is traditionally known as scientific knowledge in terms of measurement and objectivity. Studies in this field aim at raising awareness of what Aristotle called phronesis, practical wisdom. Praxis is guided by "phronesis" which often resides within the non-verbal realm; a knowing that is mainly sensed and felt. Sometimes this is referred to as silent or tacit knowledge, that which what we know but might not be able to tell.'

Schön refers to an important 'gap between artistry and its description' which 'should be given a central place to the ways practitioners learn to create opportunities for *reflection-in-action*' (Schön, 1983: 267). Like Johns, Schön focused on learning influenced by the person of the practitioner with an interest in our knowing *in* the moments.

## Key thinker – Donald Alan Schön (1930–1997)

Donald Schön is often regarded as the 'father of reflective practice'. He coined the phrase in 1983 in his book *The Reflective Practitioner*. Although this chapter will explore reflective practice with particular reference to Donald Schön's original theories, we will also look at how reflective practice has been linked to concepts such as reflexivity and critical reflection.

Donald Schön researched and wrote for over 40 years about organisational learning. He was often associated with Harvard scholar Chris Argyris, and both were influential thinkers in developing the theory and practice of reflective professional learning in the twentieth century. Schön's book *The Reflective Practitioner* (1983) challenged practitioners to reconsider the role of technical and instrumental knowledge in favour of more open, social and reflective inquiry. This thinking gained huge influence in teacher education, health professions and architectural design.

*Frame Reflection* is another well-known title by Schön, published in 1994 and co-authored with Martin Rein. Schön's theory on 'framing' challenged the way politicians and policy makers based 'framings' of social problems. Schön argued that policy making often rested on tacit, 'taken for granted' knowledge, rather than seriously considered and reflected-upon information. Schön invited managers and decision makers to move beyond a purely rational model of understanding to a more inquiring, social and reflective approach to problems.

## Reflection-in-action

Reflective practice includes a focus on how the practitioner 'shapes the [situation] and makes himself part of it' (Schön, 1983: 163). Schön's reflective practice theory revolves around the practitioner's 'reflective conversation with practice' in ways which 'includes his own contribution to it' (p. 163).

In 'real-word practice', problems are 'puzzling, troubling and uncertain' (Schön, 1983: 40) rather than presenting themselves as tidy, text-book givens. Until surprises – good or bad – come our way, our knowing-in-action tends to rely on intuitive knowing as learnt, internalised and 'embodied in the practitioner's feel for' a task. Most reflection-in-action 'hinges on surprise' (Schön, 1983: 56), and when 'practitioners reflect-in-action' they tend to 'describe their own intuitive knowing' (Schön, 1983: 276). Schön refers to skiing as an example. A scientific focus can provide an excess of information and actually paralyse rather than support progress. Questions for less paralysing replies might be 'how do you do it?' with openness for explorations like 'I move with a wavy motion' or I am 'leaning into the slope':

> Everyone who has tried to learn from a book how to ski [and knows] how difficult it can be to act from such a description ... Reflection-in-action does not depend on a description of intuitive knowing that is complete or faithful to [full] representation [...] A good coach learns to capture the complexity of action in metaphor ('Lean into the slope!') that helps to convey the performance. (Schön, 1983: 279)

Some practices offer greater space for 'action-present ... iterations and variations of actions [to] be tried' (Schön, 1983: 129). Schön refers to a 'virtual world' where the therapist 'becomes adept at his relationship with the [client] into a world of inquiry in which thoughts and feelings can be seen as sources of discovery rather than as triggers to action' (Schön, 1983: 161). He speaks about aiming to 'step into the client's shoes', whilst also emphasising a reciprocal, shared understanding based on a 'reflective contract' as will be explored in Chapter 2.

We can see this echoing with an emphasis on *intersubjectivity* as expressed in both humanistic and psychoanalytic theory. Rogers (1995: 8) describes for instance 'reciprocal experiencing' as underpinning therapy, and that it is both conscious and 'visceral', felt sharing of experiencing which underpins the therapeutic aim to listen *with* rather than *about* the other. Rogers refers to therapists aiming to hear 'the expressed ideas and attitudes from the other person's point of view' and how this, in turn, involves seeking to adopt the other's 'frame of reference to the things he is talking about' (Rogers, 1961: 332). This brings us back to the 'aesthetics' in terms of sensing and feeling, as it involves trying to 'sense how it feels to [the client]' (Rogers, 1961: 332).

Today, we can see a growing interest in Integrative Relational theory approaching the therapeutic relationship as an intersubjective space where we 'touch and are touched by the Other in multiple, often unseen ways' (Finlay, 2016: 12). Working at 'Relational Depth' (Cooper, 2013; Mearns & Cooper, 2005/2018) is often referred to as 'facilitative, healing [and] seen by participants as highly significant with an enduring positive effect, both on the therapeutic process and long after the therapy had ended' (Knox, 2008: 35). It involves 'a state of profound contact and engagement between two people in which each person is fully real with the Other, and able to understand and value the Other's experiences at a high level' (p. 54). When researched (Cooper, 2013; Knox, 2008), it is often described as something spontaneous, in the moment experienced, characterised as being immersed, free of distractions recognised as an often warm, physical, embodied – and sometimes electrifying – tingly sensation. Daniel Stern offers an illustrative example of a phenomeno-logical connection through so-called 'kairos moment' which he believes captures qualitative shifts in therapy. The jointly lived and shared experience, as described in terms of a present moment, requires that the therapist, to some degree, surrenders their framework of understanding and, in the process, abandons their 'technically accepted response'. Stern continues:

> The nature of a now moment usually demands something beyond a technically accept-able response: It demands a moment of meeting … It must be spontaneous and must carry the therapist's personal signature, so to speak … (Stern, 2004: 164)

Stern refers to the 'present moment' to describe this inter-subjective experience:

> Take, for example, the patient who suddenly sat up to look at her therapist. Right after the patient also sat up, the two found themselves looking at each other intently. A silence prevailed. The therapist, without knowing exactly what she was going to do, softened her face slowly and let the suggestion of a smile form around her mouth. She then leaned her head forward slightly and said, 'Hello'. The patient continued to look at her. They remained looking in a mutual gaze for several sec-onds. After a moment, the patient laid down again and continued her work on the couch, but more profoundly and in a new key, which opened new material. (Stern, 2004: 169)

Sedgwick referred to the meeting in '**the between**' people as necessarily involving a 'mutual transformation' (Sedgwick, 2005: 37) referred. Something happens when two people meet on this level, with an interest in bringing only themselves into the equation. Both parties are involved in a joint creation akin to what happens when two chemical mixtures result in a new, third compo-nent. In the case study below, Helen's supervisor offers a support on different levels with regard to accessing this value.

## Case Study 1.4

Helen is a 45-year-old counsellor with ten years' experience from both individual and couple work. When Helen was 16 years old, she was told that she was adopted as a baby by her grandmother. Her biological mother was Laura, whom she had considered to be her sister up to this point. Helen's supervisor was reminded of this experience during a session when Helen referred to an assess-ment of a self-referred couple seeking help at her private practice.

'I felt sorry for the husband. The wife was the ruthless kind, you know, the real bitchy type who just don't care,' concluded Helen in what came across to the supervisor as a careless way. Helen spoke louder than usual, used slang and gestures, which brought supervisor associations to a teenager. Helen had normally struck the supervisor as a reflective person who chose to consider her own reactions carefully. Her detachment from her new client stood out as unusual and the supervisor wondered if Helen communicated something from the session in both words and behaviour.

'What makes you think that the wife doesn't care?' asked the supervisor.

Helen shrugged her shoulders.

'Don't know,' she said.

'You don't know ...'

'Well, I suppose it's the whole package. You know, the type with heavy makeup. Giggly, loud, probably just thinking about herself and when to have fun next. Almost tarty ... well, insincere.'

'She seemed to have stirred some strong feelings in you ...'

'I can't stand that type of woman.'

'Can you describe what feelings you experience in her company?'

Helen shifted restlessly in her chair, she gesticulated, pulled a funny face and laughed a little.

'I just feel very sorry for him, her husband ...'

The supervisor remained silent.

'He must feel so ...' Helen shrugs her shoulder again. 'Well, so boring. So unwanted.'

'Unwanted?'

'Well, that's how you feel with those kind of women ...'

They both remained silent. Helen's body language changed, she grew still, sighed and added:

'She reminds me of my mother, the sister who went out dancing all the time ...'

Helen and her supervisor used the rest of the session to unpick the assessment session in a new light after this. Helen recognised that she assessed the couple through inappropriately tainted lenses, and she appreciated the safe space to explore 'what is what'.

## Comment

In the case study, the supervisor listens out for the therapist Helen's both spoken and unspoken references to her recent couple counselling practice. Helen's own training has also, in turn, prepared her for being open for these kinds of events, and the supervisory relationship felt safe enough for Helen to quickly pick up on the supervisor's hints and make use of the opportunity to bring blurred aspects into awareness.

## Reflection-*in*-action

The space between knowing-in-action and theory-in-action remained at the forefront for Schön's development of reflective practice. He suggests that we look at 'the inherent complexity of intuition' (Schön, 1983 279) with an interest in reflection-in and reflection-on action. Schön refers to different kinds of 'on-the-spot experiments' as outcomes of the reflections:

- The **'exploratory experiment'** involves intuition and 'getting a feeling' for something. It is characterised by a 'probing, playful activity by which we get a feeling for things [which] succeeds when it leads to the discovery of something there' (Schön, 1983: 145). Schön compares this with what a newcomer may do when wandering around a strange neighbourhood, but also something which a scientist may do first encountering and probing a strange substance to see how it will respond.
- The **'move-testing'** involves a deliberate action, taken with an end in mind; such as when a chess player's advance of a pawn to protect his queen or when the carpenter tried fastening a board across the angle of a corner when making a structure stable. The move-testing on-the-spot experiment 'is affirmed when it produces what is intended for it and negated when it does not' (Schön, 1983: 146). However, Schön continues, 'the affirmation of a move is not only Do you get what you intend? But Do you like what you get?' (Schön, 1983: 146) There is, in this sense, an ethical dimension of the experiment. Giving a sweet to a crying child might make her stop crying, but with unintended less good effects. A reflection-on-action will take in 'it's consequences as a whole' (Schön, 1983: 146).
- The third on-the-spot experiment refers to a reflection-in-action guided by **'hypothesis-testing'**. Following Schön's idea that reflective practice revolves around a practitioner's 'reflective conversation [with] how practice includes his own contribution to it' (Schön, 1983: 163), the term hypothesis testing is used differently to what scientific lens would explore based on neutrality and objectivity. My understanding of his use of it in context of therapy is in an almost interchangeable way to move-testing on-the-spot experiment. When for instance referring to 'transference', Schön refers to a hypothesis-testing experiment which includes the practitioner's focus on how s/he 'shapes the [situation] and makes himself part of it' (Schön, 1983: 163).

## Espoused theory and theory-in-use

Schön's reflection-in-action theory was proceeded by studies (Argyris & Schön, 1978) suggesting a difference for many practitioners between their 'espoused theory', or what we officially committed themselves to, and their 'theory-in-use'. An important point with this research was that the absence of the espoused theory often surprised the practitioners themselves. Argyris and Schön wrote:

> When someone is asked how he would behave under certain circumstances, the answer he usually gives is his espoused theory of action for that situation. This is the theory of action to which he gives allegiance, and which, upon request,

he communicates to others. However, the theory that actually governs his actions is his theory-in-use [with] implicit values and assumptions, often taken for granted. (Argyris and Schön, 1978: 6–7)

The reasons for this gap between 'theory-in-use' and the 'espoused theory' are many, ranging from unconscious decisions to organisational, cultural factors obscuring the practitioner's own insight. People can, for instance, become protective about their theories. Schön and Rein refer to the sociologist Gusfield's suggestions that clinicians and practitioners 'cannot afford to stand outside the framework within which action occurs' (Schön & Rein, 1994: xiii). To examine our theory in terms of a belief system among a number of possible frameworks would, in Gusfield's mind, require the clinicians to 'give up that wholehearted commitment to a single set of in beliefs that is indispensable to their effective action'. Gusfield suggested that once we begin to question our theory as only one of many possible, we begin to doubt what we are doing and possibly lose our motivations altogether. Schön disagreed and based the thinking around reflective practice on the belief that clinicians were quite capable of both working with maps and keeping an open mind, for that the maps required ongoing re-assessment in light of upcoming problems and new challenges.

## Re-framing problems: Single- and double-loop learning

Argyris and Schön's idea of single-loop and double-loop learning reflected their interest in transformative learning. The double-loop learning highlighted attitude, values and assumptions behind strategies and solutions:

- Single-loop learning is like a thermostat that learns when it is too hot or too cold and turns the heat on or off. The thermostat can perform this task because it can receive information (the temperature of the room) and take corrective action.
- Double-loop learning occurs when the error is detected and corrected in ways that involve the modification of an organisation's underlying norms, policies and objectives. (Argyris & Schön, 1978: 2–3)

A single loop is 'completed within a single coherent frame of references' (Hawkins & Shohet, 2005: 79). It concerns explicit, expressed and often officially adhered to objectives and strategies. Double looping involves aiming to make tacit, implicit assumptions explicit with an interest in critical appraisal of use of self, theory and one's socio-cultural framing. Hawkins and Shohet illustrate how double-loop learning is a fundamental position in therapy:

It is the second loop that actually digs below our questions and finds new ones. For instance, a supervisee might learn within a single loop that clients may be erratic in their attendance if a clear contract is not made, but when the learning has a double loop they may understand, for example, why they are drawn not to make a clear contract with the client who shares with them the difficulty in accepting authority. (Hawkins & Shohet, 2005: 78)

## Dialectical and transformative learning

Reflective practice is in this sense neither about tick-boxes nor about being 'navel gazing' (Bolton, 2005/2018), but is rather about moving between contrasting perspectives with transformative, integrative learning in mind. An aim for 'dialectical engagement' with contrasting perspective assumptions are underpinning aims:

> By dialectical, I mean an engagement that is ongoing and recursive, as opposed to a single ... encounter. In the process of trying to understand another, our own beliefs and assumptions are disclosed, and these assumptions, themselves, can become objects of examination and critique. (Carter & Gradin, 2001: 4)

This rests in turn on an openness for 'transformative learning' in the sense that Mezirow (2009) used the terms when engaging in 'disorienting dilemmas' which don't fit into a person's current beliefs about the world. A disorientating dilemma triggers critical reflection about something which we hold as true, valid and reliable. That involves, by definition, letting go of familiar explanatory framework which can involve stages of loss and confusion. A disorienting dilemma prompts us to reconsider our beliefs so that the new experience can fit into the rest of our worldview. Mezirow describes this in terms of *'learning that transforms problematic frames of reference to make them more inclusive, non-discriminating, reflective, open, and emotionally able to change'* (Mezirow, 2009: 18; emphasis added).

## Psychological mindedness

The 'multistructural' process of considering and connecting one's responses to client situations are, finally, significantly depending on the therapist's psychological mindedness. Klein et al. explore the meaning of psychological mindedness with the following abilities in mind:

> [Psychological mindedness involves] an interest in discovering the meaning of things, a curiosity about human motivation, a capacity for introspection, an interest in latent as well as manifest content, and a fundamental curiosity about what makes people tick. (Klein, Bernard & Shermer, 2011: 273)

Lehman (2008) highlights how transformation involves 'the development of awareness of what ... pushes us to feel and act in the way we do' (Lehman, 2008: 298). Transformative learning is, in this sense, not just about positive experience: it highlights the value of bringing negative experiences to the forefront. In Chapter 6 of this book, Biljana van Rijn will return to 'reflective knowledge' to emphasise the role of knowledge in creating *change*. Reflection supports us to explore 'forces and circumstances' which may hold us back from change, which in this book is explored in terms of personal, theoretical and socio-cultural circumstances.

## Reflection point

Can you think of a personal crisis or problem that has become an asset in your work as a therapist?

Read the case study with these questions in mind and reflect on how Sarah appears to be handling the concerns.

## Case Study 1.5

### Sarah and Pat in supervision

Sarah is a psychodynamic psychotherapist with a placement in an agency where she receives fortnightly supervision. She also practises from home. Sarah usually strikes her supervisor as an enthusiastic and inquisitive person, and it is unusual for her to feel detached from work. But Sarah struggles with a new client, Pat, who is a night-time nurse with depression as her presented problem. Sarah normally writes two sets of notes – she presents brief comments for the agency and brings verbatim transcripts into supervision where she tries to recall her sessions word by word.

This is the second time that Sarah has reported feeling distant from Pat, and she struggles with remembering enough from the session even to write notes.

'I think I just want to forget the session,' admits Sarah. 'All I can remember is how time passes really slowly; I keep looking at the watch.'

After their last session, Sarah dreamt about Pat.

'I was desperate to find somewhere to sit ... Pat expected therapy, and, well, it was embarrassing, stressful ... it felt all wrong. Wherever we went there were kids and dogs and stuff,' says Sarah. 'Even my mum was there; she just walked straight in and started to talk about something to do with the house.'

Sarah looks annoyed and distant, and the supervisor wonders if she is enacting some of the experiences in the supervision. She looks for any message, verbal or enacted, for an understanding of Sarah's experiences with Pat. Sarah seems to be lost in thought and only eventually does she resume. She says that her feelings of not 'finding a good enough space' for Pat lingered long after the dream.

'I don't even really want to talk about her now either,' observes Sarah. She admits to feeling confused; she feels detached but at the same time the work with Pat feels almost intrusive or 'too close for comfort'.

'I'd like to map out to myself what's happening ... like this,' she says and reaches for some paper. She divides the paper into a dialectical note.

*(Continued)*

'This is what she says, Pat ... and this is what I see,' explains Sarah as she notes both what and how things had been said in their last session. Pat had kept her coat on, yet said, 'I really trust you.'

'And this is your voice,' she adds to her supervisor, '... when you talked about depression as anger – you know, when I felt so sorry for her that time. Well, I've been trying to use that, but it actually just made me even more confused. You said something about not feeling sorry for her ... or not treating her like a victim, here!'

Distinguishing between what is actually said and what is done in terms of, for instance, body language, helps Sarah to explore her ambivalence. Pat's mixed messages become clearer. Sarah also realises how intrusive the supervisor's comment about 'depression as anger' has felt. The room seems crowded with voices and messages. The overriding theme, concludes Sarah, is her own issues around 'helping a helper', as she puts it to her supervisor. She is now able to explore how her own ambivalence has played into Pat's sense of unease and lack of trust. For both, the 'default position' is not to trust. Sarah has spent many years in personal therapy, but trust is an issue that returns in many disguises. Her supervisor secures space and feedback for Sarah to explore how best to deal with the issue this time around.

Shame and lack of trust are unfortunately common obstacles for therapists to keep problems to oneself, and to what extent we face and engage with these obstacles will impact our involvement with our clients. Reflecting on practice through writing can address and alleviate some of this, for instance when used before and after supervision.

## Reflective writing: We do not store, we story our experiences

Reflective writing is a term used for writing for the purpose of 'making sense of ourselves and the world' (Bolton, 2005/2018: 4). Rather than storing experiences like computers, we 'story' them, asserts Bolton. She contends that:

> Writing is different from talking; it has a power all of its own ... It can allow an exploration of cognitive, emotional and spiritual areas otherwise not accessible. (Bolton, Field, & Thomson, 2006)

Reflective writing involves 'examining our story-making processes critically, to create and recreate fresh accounts of our lives from different perspectives, different points of view and to elicit and listen to the responses of peers' (Bolton 2005/2018: 3). To question our 'story making' involves 'deconstructing' (Fook, 2002) and examining the narratives that we hold about ourselves and our world, in this case about ourselves as professional helper.

## Activity 1.3   The story of your life

This exercise is about your life story. You will be asked to write a brief piece, no more than five minutes, about a significant life event, followed by a piece about your approach to work.

- Choose a significant event or an important personal memory and write down what you remember – as associations and memories come; there is no need to think of structure or form.
- Write something in brief about you at work. Write down something which comes up from your latest session, or something general which springs to mind. Write again, as the thoughts come into your head.
- Compare the two stories. In what way do they overlap or differ? Are you presented in significantly different ways? If so, how?
- If possible, show and discuss the texts in pairs.

## Relative 'permanence' of writing

Unlike speech, writing has the benefit of allowing us to return to, linger over and reflect upon what we have constructed in our own mind. Smith referred to this as 'the relative permanence' of writing:

> Writing is an extremely efficient way of gaining access to knowledge that we cannot explore directly. It is more efficient than speaking in many respects because of its relative permanence and because we can stand back and examine it as an independent entity. (Smith, 1985: 33)

To write reflectively, it is important to demystify writing. Smith refers to writing as rather 'an extension and reflection of all our efforts to develop and express ourselves in the world around us'; it does not require esoteric skills, unusual talents or lengthy training. Writing both reflects and creates meaning; it 'helps us to make sense of [the] world and to impose order upon it' (Smith, 1985: 160). The stages in your reflective writing can be compared with what Schön refers to as moving from 'knowing-in-action' to 'knowledge-in-action'; the first being guided by internalised, learnt knowing drawn upon intuitively in the moment.

## Free writing

So, a full reflective composition is often moving from fleeting thoughts and impulsive reactions to a more structured version of events that can eventually be reflected upon and explored in terms of themes and patterns The first 'free writing' stage is often the most important. **Free associative writing involves writing without a stop**.

## Activity 1.4

- Write for 5–6 minutes.
- If you run out of words, just write 'word, word …' until a new association takes form. Relax, and allow a focus to occur – it can be a dog barking outside, a curtain moving by an open window or something relating to you, ranging from cold feet or a funny feeling when you think of something recent or upcoming.
- **How did that feel? Did anything unexpected come up?** Were you surprised, relieved – or maybe indifferent or even frustrated?

Shame and judgement are important themes in writing, and a good place to start can be to write with the prompt about 'what I wouldn't like others to know', for instance, our supervisor or sometimes our clients. In the form of (unsent) letter writing exercise, Wright stresses:

> The aim is to be creative and free in your explorations … The non-judgmental paper or screen will not be shocked … so there is no need to censor. (Wright, 2018: 122)

Wright offers numerous prompts, including starting with bodily sensations like 'if my hands/stomach/heart/nose could speak' (Wright, 2018: 44) or completing sentences like 'what I want is …' or 'thinking about that client, I …'. Wright also suggests free writing starting with 'three long, slow breaths, close your eyes …' Reflective writing ranges from assessment and journal writing to poetry; for instance, 'cut-up poetry' which incorporate metaphors, comparing for instance an aggressive boss with red wine; 'fine tannins with black cherries, lively acidity … belligerent, beating …' (Wright, 2018: 48).

## Activity 1.5    Your unsent letter to a client

Wright invites us to write an 'unsent letter to a client'. Her letter begins in a positive, polite way, but illustrates how free writing can allow uncomfortable topics to surface, as her letter continues with 'I like your humour [but] when you start talking about violence … I feel my stomach tightening … my mouth goes dry …' (Wright, 2018: 122).

- Focus on the lower area of your stomach, listen to your 'gut feeling' while thinking about some of your recently seen clients. Notice how you feel about each of them. Choose anyone who interests you, write for five minutes – starting your letter with 'Dear X …'
- Who did you choose? What feelings were involved when you chose that client? What came up when you wrote? How did that feel for you? Do you feel supported to explore your work?

## Our cultural contexts

Wright's earlier mentioned book *Reflective Writing* offers a broad approach to self-exploration. Wright draws from *'the magic of words and human imagination, the power of symbols and imagery'* to explore feelings and thoughts *'in an elaborate network of meaning and change according to cultural context and local knowledge'* (Wright, 2018: 35; emphasis added). The example below resonates with my own experiences in practising with English as a second language. In Wright's example the multilingual therapist 'Kitt' writes about his relationship to his second language, English:

'My emotions

it's like squeezing into clothes

I don't like

too small and is

too big and

too hot for summer and

too light for winter

I-am-hot-cold-small-big

all at the same time

nothing fits

me

its like I can never fully fit into myself

as if I am not longer who I was and who I was no longer part of who I am now

I can't fit find a fit with my new language

English

the English version of me doesn't fit the Danish version of me

it really hurts

and nothing fits anymore

will my Danish self ever fit my English clothes' (Kitt, in Wright 2018: 35)

### Activity 1.6   Your social context

Consider yourself in relation to language, gender or socio-cultural background. Take that aspect of you into your heading or title and write without stopping for five minutes about that.

*(Continued)*

- Discuss, if possible, in pairs what you chose and what came up when you wrote. How, if at all, might that aspect of you impact your approach to practice?

Dorothea Brande, who coined the concept of 'creative writing' in the 1930s, contends that writing is about turning ourselves and our experiences into objects of attention. The exercise below offers another angle to writing about self. It is adapted from Brande, what she calls 'a primer lesson in considering oneself objectively' (Brande, 1934/1996: 55):

- You are near a door, imagine going through that door. Turn yourself into your own object of attention from the moment you stand on the threshold.
- What do you look like, standing there? How do you walk? How do you talk? What can you say about yourself – your character, your background, your purpose – just there at just that minute? If there are people in the room whom you must greet? How do you greet them? How do they greet you?
- Try to capture your impressions of yourself in the doorway. Write without stopping for ten minutes.
- What came up? Were you surprised? Discuss, if possible, in pairs.

In Chapter 2, we will explore the 'cycle' of development for therapists. Personal development addresses questions ranging from our emotional responses to situations and persons, to our basic belief about knowledge, trustworthiness and truth.

# 2

# Personal development

## Core knowledge

Some of the following key terms will be explored:

- Personal development will be explored with your support in mind.
- Personal development is approached with interest in the developmental process of becoming a therapist who reacts as a person with emotions, thoughts and behaviour.
- This involves attending to our personal history with an interest into how this may influence how we respond to our clients.
- Supervision is approached as the first point of call for support and reflective space.

## Personal development

Personal development invites a third person perspective on ones' professional life, raising questions about how we integrate our personal experiences in our professional development and planning. What drives us and why? What may be our weaknesses and wherein lie our strengths? How will different training and career options respond to these? Personal development addresses questions ranging from our emotional responses to how we approach knowledge, trustworthiness and truth. It also, importantly, addresses what we may need in terms of personal and professional support to develop. Personal development involves a dynamic and holistic perspective on the therapist. Neuhaus concludes, 'I define personal development to include present and the past.' He refers to 'learning how to become a therapist who reacts as a person with emotions, thoughts and behaviour both inside and outside the hour' and how 'one's personal history ... may have a significant influence on the ways in which the therapist reacts' (Neuhaus, 2011: 224).

We will explore five key areas in particular:

1. Clinical supervision
2. Personal therapy
3. Creativity, reflective writing included
4. CPD
5. Research

## The 'evolution' of the helper

During the last decade, some significant research has emerged in the field of personal development for counselling and psychotherapy. Interviews, story writing and large-scale surveys from 5,000 therapists from over 20 countries (Orlinsky & Ronnestad, 2005; Ronnestad, Orlinsky, Schröder, Skovholt, & Willutzki, 2019) highlight many important overlapping themes.

In an overview of their many studies, Ronnestad, Orlinsky, Schröder, Skovholt, and Willutzki (2019) refer to 'reflective practice' as an underpinning prevention for therapists' stressful involvement.

Orlinsky and Ronnestad identified early in their studies a reported experience about a rapidly accelerated depleting cycle, which seemed to be linked to lack of emotional and theoretical support for therapists to process problems. The experience of 'effective, constructive and affirming relationships' with clients tended to be reported as a rejuvenating experience in itself (Orlinsky & Ronnestad, 2005: 169; emphasis added). These positive experiences would often trigger 'renewal of interest and optimism', which fed back into the therapeutic relationship and contributed to a 'felt importance of further development'. However, feeling unsupported and confused in stressful moments would trigger something which Orlinsky and Ronnestad called 'stressful involvement' with a 'premature closeness'. This involved 'interrupting the reflection process before the assimilation/accommodation work is completed. It is an unconscious, predominately defensively motivated, distorting process that sets in when the challenge is too great' (Orlinsky & Ronnestad, 2005: 172).

Once started, Orlinsky and Ronnestad (2005) noticed how a 'stressful cycle' quickly escalated (see Figure 2.1). Typical for the stressful involvement was a sense of 'awkwardness, insecurity and defensive rigidity' which prevented the therapists from seeking new solutions – be it in supervision, personal therapy or further training. The lack of processing opportunities at an early stage of the problem, fed into a sense of stagnation, boredom and general lack of motivation.

Skovholt and Trotter-Matthison's (2011) studies highlight, further, some important themes across therapists, looking at stages of training and practice. They explore early therapists as 'lay helpers' (such as a friend or family member) and reflect on their process to become 'professional' helpers. The section below invites you to position yourself in the development of therapy training, with your own PD (personal development) needs in mind.

## 1. The lay helper phase

A lay helper is 'a novice who helps others in a nonprofessional setting [without] any formal training in counselling ... who can be prone to problem identification, advice giving, and boundary issues' (Skovholt & Trotter-Mathison, 2011: 6). Skovholt and Trotter-Mathison continue:

> [In lay helping] there is a projection of one's own experiences and one's own solution to the life ... The lay helper often gives answers and these can have a base in the notion of common sense. There will usually not be a self-conscious or reflectivity about the helping process. (Skovholt & Trotter-Mathison, 2011: 56)

---

### Activity 2.1    Time travelling

In the following activity, you are encouraged to write for ten minutes without stopping. Continue writing from the sentence below for five minutes. If you can't think of what to write, write 'word, word' until a new associative thread comes up:

> 'I remember it was a school day, maybe a Tuesday or a Wednesday. I was sitting on my bed, looking for a sock, thinking that ...'

When you have finished:

- Trace how you are **feeling right now**.
- What came up for you?
- How old was the person you wrote about? What went on for that person, at that time? Who looked after you? What was that like?
- In what way, if at all, are there any links between the upcoming themes in your story, with how you are today: What is different, what has changed? Discuss in pairs if possible.

---

*Comments*

Some express surprise over the amount of details that comes up in the writing, like smells, sounds and other vivid memories linked to time and place.

Others comment sometimes upon how little came up. In one writing group, a member described, for instance, feeling almost paralysed, unable to write a single word. He was later able to reflect over how this actually coincided with his feeling both at home and in school at this particular time. Many describe how strong feelings return in their writing; like sadness, helplessness and loneliness or, indeed, as in some cases, excitement. One person remembers the day his mother was being hospitalised and memories from trying to make sense of all this, when he came to school, flooded back. This triggered a discussion about how many in the group were 'wounded healers' who could recall a sense of leading a double life as children with a messy household and an urge to fit in and be a 'normal' child at school. Often, the writers are surprised afterwards to recognise that the age wasn't specified and that the feeling that they had about being asked to write about themselves with a special age in mind is linked to their own way of prioritising events. In one writing group, a member said afterwards that she found it easy to write: 'It was the grey sock that did it for me' she said; and recognised only afterwards that this was in response to what had come up for her, rather than being specifically addressed in the question.

## 2. The beginning student phase

This first stage of training 'signals a time of high dependency, vulnerability, and anxiety in trainees as they seek out the "right way" ... [often] modelled by expert clinicians'. Trotter-Mathison, Skovholt et al. highlight the temptation to elevate the anxiety either by retreating or through 'clinging onto' one way of understanding the complex reality:

> There has been an increase in understanding the complexity of the professional world ... If the anxiety is too strong the student may retreat. Leaving the field or rigidly clinging on to one way of understanding reality (one theoretical approach), are two retreat styles that reduce the anxiety but, unfortunately, also reduce the capacity for cognitive complexity, a long-term key to senior expertise ... (Skovholt & Trotter-Mathison, 2011: 59)

A key difference from lay-helping to early student phase is the 'self-consciousness or reflectivity about the helping process' (Skovholt & Trotter-Mathison, 2011: 56).

## 3. The advanced student phase

This stage involves an increased focus onto the reactions of the therapist. Skovholt and Trotter-Mathison suggest further that students at this stage typically 'value time not only to discuss skill development, but also to process how they are feeling about their experiences, supervision, and their own development' (Skovholt & Trotter-Mathison, 2011: 6). It is usually a rather 'raw' stage of the development.

Trainees are 'likely to feel anxious and overwhelmed', as Orlinsky and Ronnestad point out, suggesting that 'educators need to recognise this and structure the learning situation so that anxiety-related emption can be kept to a level where they can be mastered' (Orlinsky & Ronnestad, 2005: 185).

For counsellors and psychotherapists, the boundary between our professional and personal selves is often fluid. Folkes-Skinner, Elliott and Wheeler (2010: 91) stress that 'all education demands change' but how therapy training usually involves particularly deep changes. They remind us that 'trainee therapists are required to change not only their thinking and to develop new skills, but also adapt aspects of their personality'. Furthermore, Folkes-Skinner et al. assert that:

> [Therapy training] is a potentially disturbing personal journey that requires a deconstruction of the self to meet the need of clients. This change process appears to be influenced and supported by experiential learning exercises such as role-play and group supervision, but may be fundamentally driven by experiences working with real clients. (Folkes-Skinner et al., 2010: 91)

Skovholt and Trotter-Mathison (2011: 80) suggest that 'at work, counsellors, therapists, teachers and health professions live in an ocean of emotional distress'. They found that many novice practitioners experienced an acute level of stress which they often felt ashamed to talk about. In his reflections on therapy as a profession, Kottler captures for many of us an underlying dichotomy in our work:

> Being a therapist is truly a life-long journey, one in which we accompany others on a road towards enlightenment or peace or salvation. [However] our journey to become therapists began for most of us, not with the urge to save the world or help people, but rather to save ourselves. (Kottler, 2011: 1)

## Case study 2.1

Julie is in her second year of diploma training in integrative counselling. She is married to Paul, an accountant, with one daughter who is in her second year at university. Julie has previously worked in childcare. 'I have always liked looking after people,' says Julie. Both her parents are dead. She is close to her younger brother who is a GP and, as Julie puts it, has always been the 'golden boy' of the family. She has recently started her clinical placement at her local GP surgery. Yesterday she was advised about a new client enquiry from a woman, Alice, with bereavement as her presented problem. Julie felt both nervous and excited about seeing her new client. She felt sorry for her – Julie knew only too well what it was like to lose someone you love.

However, during their first session, Julie is struck by Alice's confidence and neat appearance. Alice is a psychologist, who asks 'probing' questions about Julie's qualifications. Halfway through the session, she asks if there is someone else whom she can see – she is concerned whether Julie is experienced enough to deal with her issues. Julie leaves the session feeling deskilled, angry and sad.

*(Continued)*

She tells her supervisor afterwards that the client seems unreasonable and would be too difficult for her to work with. When the supervisor encourages Julie to describe her feelings, she answers that she feels 'bullied'.

'What's it like for you to be bullied?'

'Well, you're made to feel rubbish, aren't you; useless, like you can't do anything right and like no one really cares about you.'

'Is this the first time you've experienced that kind of feeling?'

'No! I used to feel like this a lot. I wasn't exactly bullied, but my brother was bossy ... he always thought he knew best, it used to really get up my nose!'

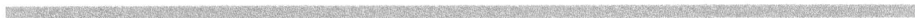

*Comment*

Julie and her supervisor are able to explore how Julie's fears about not being good enough might have come into play during her session with Alice. Julie returns to the moment when she started to feel uncomfortable and recognises feeling deskilled at quite an early stage of their conversation. Perhaps, muses her supervisor, there had been a collusion taking place? Maybe both Julie and Alice had a fear of failure? Or maybe Julie's fears triggered something in Alice; perhaps a dread for being 'too much' for people? Julie and her supervisor explore how Alice might feel turning for help, being a 'helper' herself.

## 4. The novice professional phase

This is a phase when 'therapists learn to increasingly incorporate their own personalities into treatment', as Skovholt and Trotter-Mathison put it (2011: 173). This can be an unsettling experience. The ambiguity of emotions and meaning-making processes returns as an inevitable dimension of our work. The constraints of the training institute are left behind 'but in their wake, therapists often discover that graduate school has not prepared them as well as hoped [for an] independent practice'. To develop, as Klein, Bernard and Shermer (2011: 278) put it, 'skilful use of self' characterised by self-awareness and a 'know-thyself' principle personal therapy, supervision, readings and peers become essential means of support.

## 5. The experienced professional phase

This is a phase when Skovholt and Trotter-Mathison (2011) note 'a focus on establishing authenticity'. They suggest that experienced professionals '*nearly universally recognise the centrality of the therapeutic relationship in contributing to client change. They also become increasingly comfortable with the necessary ambiguity in counselling interactions*' (Skovholt & Trotter-Mathison, 2011: 6; emphasis added).

## 6. The senior professional phase

At this stage, 'self-confidence is often tempered by acknowledgement of the real limitations of their impact on client change with an increased focus on the client as hero' (Skovholt & Trotter-Mathison, 2011: 6). The senior therapist has typically worked for 20 years or more and often builds 'a practice on their own authenticity, idiosyncratic approaches to the field'.

---

### Activity 2.2    Your stages and involvement cycles

* Take some time to consider each of the stages of development addressed above. What issues resonate particularly with you? **In which phase of the therapist's journey would you position yourself today?**
* Explore the components of a stressful cycle in Figure 2.1. How might your career stage and overriding issues in practice overlap? What kind of support have you got, and what might you benefit from having more of right now?

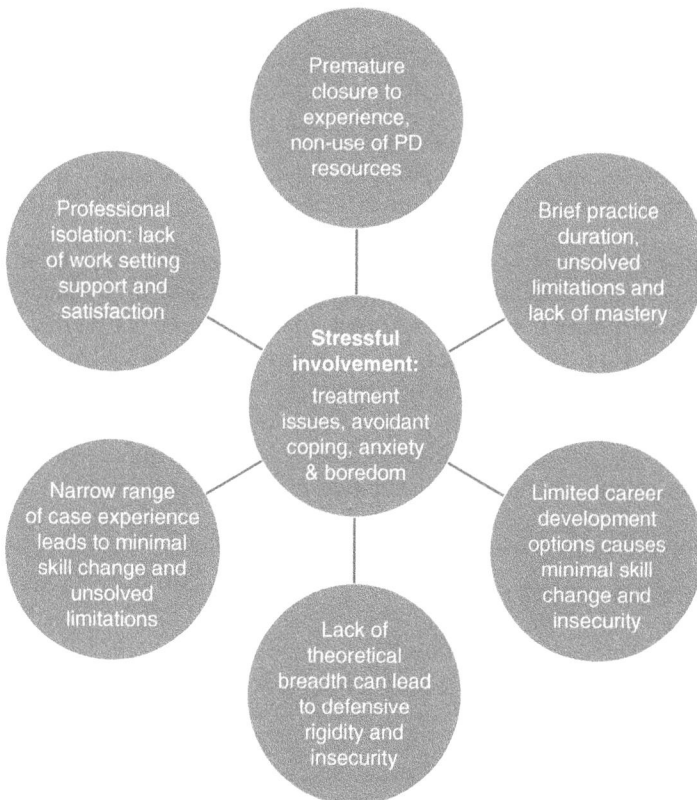

---

Premature closure to experience, non-use of PD resources

Professional isolation: lack of work setting support and satisfaction

Brief practice duration, unsolved limitations and lack of mastery

**Stressful involvement:** treatment issues, avoidant coping, anxiety & boredom

Narrow range of case experience leads to minimal skill change and unsolved limitations

Limited career development options causes minimal skill change and insecurity

Lack of theoretical breadth can lead to defensive rigidity and insecurity

*Figure 2.1*   Components in the stressful cycle, adapted from Orlinsky and Ronnestad's (2005) research into 5,000 therapists' experiences from work

We referred earlier to the importance of feeling supported to reflect emotionally and theoretically over occurring problems. Did therapy come up as a support in your reflection above?

Orlinsky and Ronnestad (2005) found that therapists rated personal therapy highly across the borders. Regardless of modality, therapists expressed appreciation of their own therapy, both in moments of distress and for a more general sense of growth:

> At every career level, personal therapy was ranked as one of the most important sources of positive influence on therapists' current development. Moreover, personal and professional growth was cited by our therapists as the leading reason for seeking therapy ... Therapists in general clearly are well aware of the benefits that personal therapy offers; four-fifths of those in our study had at least one course of therapy. (Orlinsky & Ronnestad, 2005: 199)

## Gaining insights into vulnerability

An ability to *trust* is something which we tend to encourage our clients to explore and develop. It is therefore clearly important for us. Klein et al. (2011) refer to 'trust' as an essential part of the therapist's learning experience. The therapist needs to trust others to fully engage with their clients and to, for instance, risk personal exposure and vulnerability. Klein et al. write:

> [P]eople who have been damaged and have not successfully worked through these experiences often lack this ability [to trust]. A successful therapeutic relationship is one in which patient and therapist learn to trust one another. (Klein et al., 2011: 273)

The therapist's own personal therapy is often regarded as one of the most important training experiences within both psychoanalytic and humanistic therapy. It brings the opportunity to rebuild our trust. Many helpers 'set themselves' up for a cycle of depletion by avoiding help and support and maintain the image of 'I always need to be there for others'. Personal therapy can then be difficult for trainee therapists. Adams' (2014) international research into therapists' personal lives lead her to conclude there is an often occurring, unhelpful 'myth of the untroubled therapist' – the title of her rich and accessible book.

---

### Reflection point

- What is your experience of trust?
- What is your experience of dealing with trust in personal therapy?

If possible, discuss in pairs.

---

Personal therapy brings an invaluable awareness of how vulnerable one can feel as a client, how confusing it can seem at first with time limited slots and just how difficult it actually is to change old patterns.

**Case Study 2.2**

Millie is on her third year of training.

'I have some issues,' said Millie when she first began her personal therapy, as part of the training. She told her therapist Margot about having been sexually abused by her father between the age of 5–11. She said she felt that she had dealt with the issue in therapy before and hoped to be able to 'focus on other things now,' she said she 'wanted to move on'.

Millie is cheerful, engaging and exceptionally neat when she does turn up. She has, however, got a tendency to cancel sessions with short notice. When eventually addressing her irregular attendance, Millie responds with anger. She says that she feels abused by 'unreasonable' requirements on the trainees. She is fed up with having to work voluntary and pay for her own therapy, which she doesn't see any need for anymore anyway. She cancels her next session but agrees to come for a final session to say goodbye.

Millie brings a dream from the night before. In the dream, she moved slowly in circles around the father who sat on a bed with a 'blanket over his thing'. In the dream, his presence felt like a magnet which Millie did all to resist, until she eventually caught sight of a door.

'I felt so happy, so very relieved,' began Millie and grew quiet. Margot notices that she is crying.

'But when I got out onto the street, I realised that I couldn't speak to anyone. I walked up and down the streets, they were crowded with people, but I got this sick, kind of sinking feeling in my stomach.'

Millie reflects over how she 'knew' in her dream that she would never be able to connect with anyone about her experiences; it was only her father who would really understand. In her dream she had returned to the room where she'd known her father had been waiting for her.

Millie and Margot remain silent for quite some time. Eventually Millie says,

'I think what I hadn't really realised until now, it just how impossible it has seemed to get help from outside.'

They agreed to continue the therapy, with a renewed focus on trust and the difficulties in letting go of the shame and the sense of exclusivity which was fostered in her abusive relationships.

---

**Activity 2.3**

Alice Miller asserts that the therapist's curiosity, empathy and 'powerful antennae' indicate 'that as a child he probably used to fulfil other people's needs and repress his own' (1997: 19). Miller links curiosity with hyper vigilance and lack of trust and addresses the need of 'working through' issues of this kind before we make helping others into our profession. Miller continues:

*(Continued)*

> If we never consciously lived through this despair and the resulting rage and have therefore never been able to work through it, we will be in danger of transferring this situation, which then would remain unconscious, onto our patients. (Miller, 1997: 20)
>
> - What is trust for you? Where does this negative or positive idea of trust stem from? Return to the writing exercise about the 'sock'. Are there any links or connections?
> - What stands out most to you, at this point, with regard to what might have been a particularly significant experience in your life? Could you identify separate incidents, or maybe recognise particular themes which have affected you, such as bereavement or illnesses within the family? Separations? Depressions? Upheavals, such as moving houses or countries? Or?
> - How might this experience impact the way you react to (certain) clients – either in a good or bad way, as a strength or a weakness, or perhaps both?

## 'Recycling' negative experiences as means of transformative learning

Many studies (Bager-Charleson, 2010; Miller, 1997; Page, 1999; Sedgwick, 2005) highlight the asymmetry involved in helping relationships. When working with vulnerable people, it is important to consider the 'darker' sides to the motivations behind choosing a philanthropic career. The Jungian analyst Guggenbuhl-Craig writes:

> People are most cruel when they can use cruelty to enforce the 'good'. We must refrain from playing the part of someone who never falls into the shadows and must be prepared to admit our mistakes with this regard ... An honest analyst will realise with horror from time to time that in his daily work he has been acting exactly like an unconscious quack and false prophet. (Guggenbuhl-Craig, 1991: 73, 113)

Sussman (1992) has conducted one of the most detailed studies of therapists' motivations. He suggests that 'an important determinant of the desire to practice psychotherapy involves the attempt to come to terms with one's own psychological conflicts'. In all of his 14 interview cases, Sussman (1992: 180) found signs of disturbance in one form or another. Some of them are reflected in the categories with quotes, below:

- Narcissistic needs: 'I was not allowed to be competent at home.'
- Aggrandises ego-ideal: '[I was thinking about becoming a priest]. Within [our] catholic church, to become a priest is the highest achievement.

Priests are the most grand, powerful, important figures. They get to wear beautiful vestments, smell of incense and hear confessions, conduct masses and offer communion. [Therapists are also important figures who people turn to with their confessions.]'

- Exhibitionism: 'I think that I have lots of actress in me that's frustrated at this point'
- Masochistic tendencies: '[I am being] used as an instrument which is smashed against the wall, thrown out of the window, kicked ... [laughs] made to feel enormously sad. Just the enormous range of emotions I get subjected to on a daily basis in my body, mind, soul has the accumulative effect over the years of being a container for all that intense emotion.'
- Problems with family members: 'I think my mother was full of loss and self-absorbed.'
- Voyerism: 'I thought that might be a very interesting part of the work, a sort of private, secret chamber of therapist and patient that really wasn't so different from sharing your secrets with a priest.'

## Motivations to practice

Becoming a psychotherapist involves indeed 'an arduous training, significant expense and uncertain career prospects' (McBeath, 2019), but more and more people are nevertheless choosing to enter this profession. Alistair McBeath (2019) performed an on-line survey which was completed by over 540 practising psychotherapists into motivations for becoming a therapist. The respondents acknowledged the significance of personal trauma and their experience of therapy as motivating factors in seeking to join the psychotherapy profession. More subtle threads of meaning were empathy and respect for clients, and how most experienced therapists seemed to have found other more personal qualities within themselves for effective therapy. A significant majority agreed that 'unconscious' elements were active in their choice to become a therapist and, somewhat in contradiction, the survey sample was evenly split as to whether it was likely that they were not 'fully aware' of their motivations to become a psychotherapist. McBeath's survey with 540 practising psychotherapists also showed that practising therapists are more inclined to reference parts of themselves as being important for effective therapy rather than any particular technique or modality. Only two respondents out of the total of 540 referenced 'modality' as an attribute of being an effective therapist. Similarly, the word 'theory' only appeared twice. Two comments seemed to capture the notion that the personal attributes of the therapist are more important than adherence to theory or technique. In other words, therapists 'unequivocally' talked about themselves and their capacity to be with clients, rather than about theory, modalities or technique. McBeath (2019) writes:

> In terms of what were considered to be the key attributes of an effective therapist – 'empathy', 'good at listening', 'respect for client' and 'being non-judgemental' were closely grouped popular choices. These and 'accepting uncertainty' were ahead of

'use of theoretical knowledge'. As shown by t-test comparisons significantly fewer of the most experienced therapists (12+ years) chose 'empathy' as a key attribute compared to other length of service groups. This most experienced group also recorded significantly more free text comments than any other group. (McBeath, 2019: 380)

## Good versus bad?

The motives for becoming a therapist can sound sinister. Sussman refers to research using the phrase 'psychological cannibalism' for a therapist's sublimated 'wish for incorporation' (1992: 149). In an inquiry of our own (Bager-Charleson, 2010), the literature about therapists' motivations seemed to suggest for psychotherapy an otherwise uncharacteristic split between good and bad therapists. There were the beautiful accounts of therapeutic practice offered by humanistic and some analytical therapists on the one hand. Buber (1947) and Rogers (1995) refer for instance to sparkling encounters and I-Thou moments 'without which we are not really living as human beings' (Rogers, 1995: 14). Jung (cited in Sedgwick, 2005) speaks about the 'alchemic bath' where the therapist and the client are able to create gold together. Psychoanalytic writers and certain other analytic therapists, such as Guggenbuhl-Craig (1991) and Miller (1981), support, on the other hand, Sussman's (1992) emphasis about the dark sides of therapists' motivations. Here, the motivations revolve predominantly around the therapist being caught in the only role he or she knows – i.e. the helper role. The career becomes, in this way, easily a matter of escaping, displacing and sublimating own wishes and unmet needs. When approaching a large group of therapists through an earlier questionnaire into therapists' motivations for practice, this dichotomy between 'good' and 'bad' motivations was at the back of our mind (Bager-Charleson, 2010). We distributed a questionnaire to 280 therapists and received 238 replies. The survey involved the following question: 'Why did you choose to be a therapist?' with six options for reply:

1. I have always been interested in people.
2. I enjoy the analytical, investigative element of therapy most.
3. The flexible working hours were essential when considering a career.
4. I believe that my own childhood influenced my choice of career.
5. A crisis in later life brought me into therapy and raised my interest in working as a therapist myself.
6. None of the above resonates with me; instead I chose to work as a therapist because of the following reason(s) ...

There was a majority of reference to personal crisis in the replies. In response to the survey, 70 per cent cited either a childhood (4) or later-life (5) 'crisis' as the trigger for becoming a therapist (Figure 2.2).

**Why I Chose To Be a Therapist**

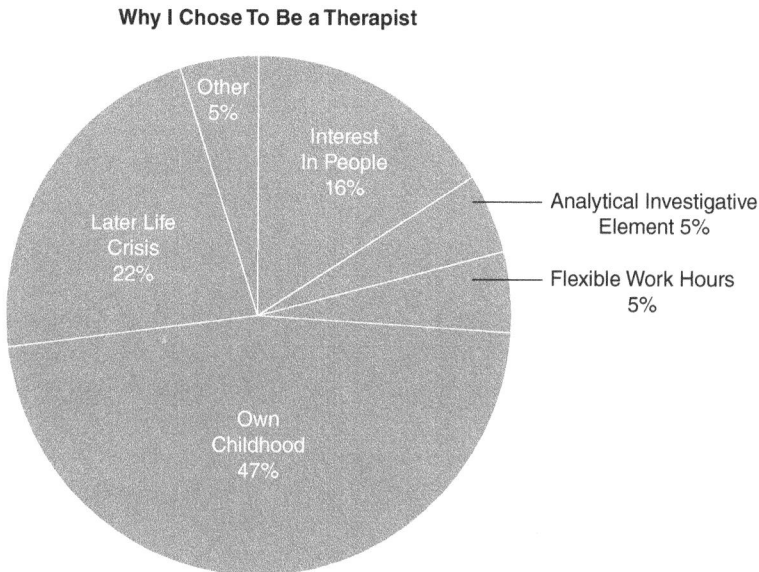

*Figure 2.2*   Responses to a survey from 238 counsellors and psychotherapists, arranged over six categories (Bager-Charleson, 2010)

---

## Activity 2.4

- Why have you chosen to become a therapist?
- Which of the themes in the questionnaire resonates most with you?

---

Some therapists replied with both childhood and adult crises. References were made to how negative childhood experiences often affects the way we are equipped to deal with further adult crises. One therapist felt that this experience has made her extra sensitive for clients who struggle with their own strong emotions:

> We never ever spoke about feelings when I grew up. This left me feeling very inadequate for many years. I felt odd for having emotions which of course made the death of my partner extra difficult to deal with. I find again and again that clients have these kind of problems; it is as if they think they are going mad for having strong feelings. My own experience of that has made me extra sensitive to that, I think.

Several therapists referred to how their own personal therapy has helped them to challenge old, narrow constructs about themselves and others. One therapist wrote about how he 'realised in therapy just how abusive my upbringing had been':

> I came from a very angry household ... Without really knowing why at the time I decided never to have children myself. My partner at the time really wanted children, and it was this that brought us into couple therapy. Our marriage ended in spite of it, and I see that as mainly my problem ... To cut a long story short, I realised in therapy just how abusive my upbringing had been. I have been in therapy for six years, and I feel ready to move on. I'd like to give something back, and I feel that I can do that through my own work with kids now.

One therapist elaborates on the combination of (1) interest in people and (5) an adult crisis:

> Mine is a mixture of 1 and 5. An initial general curiosity, about how people ticked, and human behaviour. This was intensified when I found I was unable to have children.

A curiosity in relationships and in 'how people tick' was referred to by several therapists. One therapist writes about how her interest in relationships was nourished by witnessing her sisters becoming mothers:

> I became increasingly interested in my sisters' different styles of parenting, their parent/child interactions and the children's behaviour. As an observer, supporter and, often, agony aunt to my sisters, I felt a need to understand child behaviour and parent interaction and wanted to know how things went wrong and what parents could do.

For some, more factors than two were included. The therapist below refers to a combination of an interest in people, personal childhood experiences and an adult event/crisis:

> I have marked three (1, 4, 5) criteria ... It was important in my family to have an 'interesting' career. Something that seemed worthwhile ... I have always been interested in people and psychology ... A careers assessment that I underwent at a time when I had dropped out and was entirely uninterested in any career suggested psychology and social work. It was a crisis – the breakdown of my first marriage – that got me to therapy in the first place. I found it exciting and fascinating; I've been passionate about therapy ever since.

## Common features

The inquiry which grew out of our own personal inquiry does not qualify for any grand conclusion regarding the total population of psychotherapists. It does, however, contribute with an insight into how often therapists used the term 'crisis' in a positive sense. In most cases, 'crisis' is referred to in terms of something of an 'eye opener', as illustrated below:

- 'When I lost my job, my world turned upside down. I am glad now that it made me look at the world differently. I value other things now. My own personal therapy changed my outlook on life.'

- 'I would have answered (1) if you asked me at the beginning of my training! I see now that it was more about vigilance ... in the beginning, I just felt I was cut out for this kind of job. I would take in everything in the room and my supervisor would tell me that I was being so very emotionally sensitive and astute. But really, I was frightened. My own therapy helped me to recognise that.'
- 'The bereavement counselling opened my eyes to a completely different way of being. I was used to sales and that sort of thing. Counselling opened up a whole new world for me, very different from sales. But it was also through my own counselling that I realised what a secondary place emotions used to have in our household.'
- 'I was fortunate enough to adopt ... As each year passed, things seemed to get worse and the strain of caring for one of the children was having a negative effect on the whole family. I was determined not to allow the placement to break down but the strain of holding things together had become overwhelming and I became stressed. This is when I sought counselling. I found it an immensely enlightening and enriching experience and from the very first session I wanted to be a counsellor too.'

There is, perhaps not surprisingly, a mixture of reasons in the therapists' accounts of why they chose to become therapists. It seems difficult, if not inappropriate, to imply a split between 'good' versus 'bad' motives. The uniting theme seems instead to be the 'eye opening' factor. Whether linked to a childhood event or an adult crisis, the personal experience of therapy had an impact on not only the therapist's choice of career but also on their relationships, family and/or general outlook on life.

The previously mentioned Jungian analyst Sedgwick (2005) stresses that the therapist's wound or 'pathology' is neither altogether good nor altogether bad. It is not so much a question about what has happened as how the event and experience is being known and utilised. Sussman's study (1992: 249) supports this thinking. He highlights how the success a wounded therapist may achieve is linked to his or her ability to reflect, having learnt from one's own suffering:

> Not everyone who has suffered and can identify with emotional suffering in others will be an effective therapist. These characteristics must be coupled with the following features: the capacity to control such identifications; the experience of having learned from one's own suffering, and thereby having matured; and the capacity for synthesising pleasurable, as well as painful, life experiences.

## Activity 2.5

Personal development involves a dynamic and holistic perspective on the therapist. It involves focusing on prior learning with an interest in how experiences

*(Continued)*

directly and indirectly can affect our thoughts, feelings and behaviour with our clients. Neuhaus (2011) suggests that

- '**past** refers to one's **personal history** (e.g., life span development, identity development and family relationships) that may have a significant influence on the ways in which the therapist reacts [today]', and
- '**present** refers to **the developmental process of learning how to become a therapist** who reacts as a person with emotions, thoughts and behaviour both inside and outside the hour (p. 224, my marking).

Explore your motivation for practice, with Neuhaus personal development aspects in mind.

# 3

# Your support and development

**Core knowledge**

Some of the following key terms will be explored:

- Personal development will remain a topic
- We will explore supervision and its role in the developmental process of becoming a therapist who reacts as a person with emotions, thoughts and behaviour

## Being supported

We explored motivations for practice in the previous chapter, suggesting that the idea of transforming experiences into something 'useful' often underpins personal development.

Lehman highlights how transformation involves 'the development of awareness of what ... pushes us to feel and act in the way we do'. As part of this growing awareness, old beliefs and previously held values become tested and challenged (2008: 208). Lehman continues:

> [W]e develop a sense of ownership for what lies within our repertoire of professional actions. The transformation process includes the realisation of multiple truths and perspectives for every situation and brings into consciousness the choices that are made in the process of interpreting lived experiences. (Lehman, 2008: 298)

Transformative learning is in this sense not just about positive experience, it highlights the value of bringing negative experiences to the forefront. We have, however, also explored obstacles for finding the right support for these processes. Ladany, Mori and Mehr conclude for instance that 'nondisclosure by trainees appears to be a frequent and normative aspect of supervision' (2012: 31). Their study of trainee nondisclosure indicates that 'within a single supervision session, 84.3% of trainees withheld information from their supervisors'. Issues which trainees chose to keep to themselves were often related to the trainee's

- negative perception of supervision;
- personal life concerns;
- feelings of professional inadequacy.

Not surprisingly, Ladany, Mori and Mehr stress that 'it appears that trainees would be more willing to disclose information if the supervision environment was less anxiety-provoking' (2012: 41). The supervisory relationship should, assert Frawley-O'Dea and Sarnat (2001), contain the supervisee's regressions and dissociations if and when they occur.

## Case study 3.1

### Sarah and her personal development group

Sarah dreads her personal development groups. As a psychotherapist in placement, she attends her process group fortnightly – each time with clammy hands and a dry mouth. At the start she tried to be helpful and made friendly attempts to dispel the oppressive silence. 'Is it just me who thinks the silence is a waste of time?' she volunteered, but was met by a humiliating and disorientating silence. Over time she learned to avoid attention, which seems to have made her even more of a target. Last time, a group member accused her of thinking she was better than anyone else: 'You remind me of a classmate,' he said, 'She'd be all neat and nice and tidy and make the rest of us feel like shite' Sarah was baffled. 'I don't think you mean it,' said another peer with a tone of pity which stung even more, 'You remind me of my mother who always relied on others to do the work'.

Since then Sarah's heart had begun to pound each time she wanted to speak out.

'It sounds like some of the group members find your silence hurtful', said the facilitator at their final session before Christmas. Sarah told her therapist about it, at their final session: 'It was the *way* he had said it, kindly – as if he really cared', she said. Her therapist smiled, then she broke into a huge, almost joyous, smile whilst holding Sarah's gaze for a long time during a warm, companionable silence.

Sarah was thinking about it all Christmas. The idea of mattering to someone. Just the thought of it felt new. She considered it, kind of 'tried it on' as she went about her regular tasks over Christmas. One day – when she was by the sink washing up, she looked out of the window and met her own reflection in the dark. The therapist and the facilitator felt almost present, as if they were there right next to her. Still washing up, she considered the world with them as a backdrop, experiencing it as somewhere where people could help and support her instead of being threatening and demanding. She brought this new sense of trust with her to the PPD group after Christmas, and almost immediately felt a shift.

'It's really great to hear how you feel. I want to thank you for sharing all this', said one group member when she told about her Christmas. Another group member began to cry, 'It means so much to me to hear this' said another.

Sarah returned to her therapist, exploring what had happened. She was able to tell the group how they had terrified her. She had been the youngest of five, she explained, used to drifting off to the droning voices of her siblings as they showed off, told stories, and laughed – at best, when she tried to say anything. Usually no one even heard her. Sarah continued exploring, both in the group and in her personal therapy how it had felt to be used to being silent, only finding a voice through asking, helping and cheering up others.

## Supervision is only as good as we allow it to be

Supervision is every therapists' first point of call. This section's title is borrowed from the earlier mentioned Marie Adams' research, resulting in the book titled *The Myth of the Untroubled Therapist* (2014). There may be only one basic rule, says Adams: 'If you don't want to bring it to supervision, you probably should' (2014: 117). She also offers an illustrative description of supervision, which resonates with my own experience:

> The supervisor relationship is like a Petri dish, toxic cultures of shame and vulnerability often fusing into defensive mulch. (Adams, 2014: 114)

Adams' study resonates with other recent findings suggesting that shame and lack of trust are regretfully, as suggested, common obstacles for therapists keeping problems to themselves. To what extent we face and deal with these obstacles will impact our involvement with our clients. Supervision is provided to ensure standards and enhance quality and creativity. It is a specialised form of professional mentoring provided for practitioners to enable sustainability and resilience of the work being undertaken.

## What should I look for in a supervisor?

Supervision is a unique relationship where you will need to feel comfortable to bring issues ranging from the wellbeing of your clients to concerns relating to your own personal and professional development. Questions to address, directly or indirectly, with a potential supervisor will therefore vary from ethical to emotional issues, for instance:

- Do your theoretical frameworks overlap and complement each other?
- What supervisory experiences and qualifications does your supervisor hold?
- What ethical framework does s/he adhere to?
- What experience does s/he have of working with the client group you work with?
- Do you feel comfortable and relaxed?
- Do you feel able to be honest and open?
- Does the supervisor seem interested in what you have to say?
- Are your questions being answered? Do you feel understood?
- Are you learning anything new?
- Does the supervisor inspire and facilitate your learning about both self and others?

Adams' study highlighted how we often forget to look at the supervisor relationship as a relationship. Our feelings and the way we act on them are important learning points for both ourselves and our supervisors. Looking for 'right' supervisors can often mean that we look for someone who thinks we are 'right'. Adams encourages us to avoid looking for 'collusion' and to be open for supervision that allows us to be 'wrong'. The supervisor's 'role is to explore ... feelings of shame, exposing ourselves to difficult counter-transference issues; erotic attraction and sexual fantasies, anger, dislike, visceral hatred, boredom ... [and] to delve into their meaning and find a way to understand, rather than to act upon them (Adams, 2014: 117).

## Group supervision

Peer supervision groups and personal development groups can be both especially valuable and challenging. Adams highlights the value of group supervision in providing peer support and multiple angles to our issues. However, 'as within a healthy therapy group, the group dynamic is exactly what helps to bring about a change of perspectives' (Adams, 2014: 115). We spoke earlier about how transformation typically involves loss, and often involves a considerable amount of upset before new framings begin to replace the previous ones. Adams reminds us, for instance, how 'personal pathology always play out [and can be] enacted. The group format allows the "rescuer" to show himself, along with the "pragmatist" and the "controller" ... "victims" don't escape, nor do elements of grandiosity' (Adams, 2014: 115).

## Activity 3.1

Return to your earlier writing about standing by a door.

- How does that overlap or differ from how you regard yourself in peer groups?
- How might you describe your role in terms of Adams' descriptions: a rescuer, a victim or do you tend to adopt another part in the group?
- Can you talk about that in the group?
- What might come in the way?

## Group writing

Reflective writing groups can help to delve deeper into the therapists' biography, theory and socio-cultural context. The earlier mentioned survey into Therapists' Motivation (Bager-Charleson, 2010) was an example of a peer–supervision group that incorporated writing as part of the processing. Reflective writing groups are by definition a form of research, or perhaps better put: re–searching. Reflective writing encourages us to revisit experiences and search through events again with new perspectives in mind. The more transdisciplinary such a re-search can be, the better. Some of our key learnings follow below.

A reflective writing group will be successful to the extent that its members are able to commit to a genuine attempt to understand where the other is coming from. A reflective writing group relies on trust in order to work. Reading others' texts can be as important as writing one's own. Knowing that someone will read the texts we are writing can improve, stimulate and give us a purpose to write. But is can also cause the kind of premature closure which was described earlier with reference to Orlinsky and Ronnestad (2005), in context of the stressful cycle. Reflective writing groups rest on the aim to *understand* each other rather than trying to prove a point, convince or in other ways manipulate the other.

Offering praise is an essential part of the process – being too critical of one's own writing is a common problem, which prompts many to think that they simply cannot write at all. Combating this inner criticism is fundamental for the writing to flow, and for a writing group to sustain. There will usually be general questions to attend. The reader may give their feedback on overriding purpose: What is the text about, to the reader? Who is in it? What happens? What is its theme? How has the writer chosen to arrange and present these themes? There is no 'right' in the reading, on the basis of being technically right. It is a bit like holding up a mirror to the writer and his or her text, saying: 'this is what I see – is this what you intended and wanted the readers to see?' As suggested, the clearer the writer is with regard to what he wants feedback on, the better.

Apart from the obvious interest in writing, this group was created with a relatively open agenda in mind. Therapy was for each of us a second, in some cases third, career. We enjoyed our work, but also needed a personal development group within which we could discuss post-training related disappointments and unexpected hardships.

## Activity 3.2

Have you got access to a personal development or general peer group support? If not, who could you consider instigating one with? And what type of issues would you like to feel free to explore in particular right now, with peers?

## Does supervision help you to reflect?

Reflection is, thus, an invaluable aspect of reflective practice. It helps us to loop back on our practice with questions like 'why did I respond like I did?'; 'what impact do I have on others?'; 'why does this keep happening for me?', etc. We usually need both trust and inspiration to explore such questions.

## Parallel processes

Frawley-O'Dea and Sarnat (2001: 117) emphasise that supervisory processes are about co-creating patterns during the supervision session, rather than assuming that the supervisor 'knows' the 'truth'. To explore ones' own reactions to our clients is not only a cognitive process, stress Frawley-O'Dea and Sarnat (2001) in the relational model. As therapists, we need places where we can acknowledge and connect with experiences that so far only have been around for us on an 'acting out' level. The supervisory relationship should, assert Frawley-O'Dea and Sarnat (2001), contain the supervisee's regressions and dissociations as they occur. As illustrated in the case study below, supervision should allow for unconscious means of mirroring either the client's process at the time or 'as something that she [the therapist] felt vulnerable to within herself' (Frawley-O'Dea & Sarnat, 2001: 134).

## Case study 3.2

Aida is an experienced integrative counsellor whom Marcus, her supervisor, usually finds considerate and insightful. There is something different about Aida today though. She speaks rapidly about the beautiful weather and has commented on Marcus's 'lovely curtains' twice. Marcus is reminded of the feeling he has when watching his three-year-old girl racing around in a slightly overtired state. Aida's 'joy' makes him nervous. He wonders if she is enacting something that has not yet been formulated into words.

'I'd like to talk about a new client today', chirps Aida, 'He's called Dan.' She starts on a detailed bibliographic account of Dan.

Marcus notices that he is beginning to feel tired; he is almost struggling to keep his eyes open. He reflects over how this can happen to him when there are too many conflicting messages in the room.

'He's got a very important job at the hospital. I think he's above the status of a consultant; you know, when they stop being called a doctor and take on the mister again.'

Aida goes on to discussing his family situation, and explains how Dan's wife 'never understood him'. Marcus wants to interrupt her flow, but finds no entrance.

'We settled on quite specific targets. Dan thinks that we should …' she continues.

Marcus finds himself to raising his voice to make himself heard.

'How do you feel in the room with the client?'

Aida looks taken aback. She grows quiet.

'Good …' she begins with a lower voice: 'It's good when he's pleased.' She looks pensive, and continues:

'But … to be honest, I think I am a bit worried about upsetting him'.

Marcus' intervention turns the focus onto Aida's feelings. She turns to a third person perspective on the dynamic between the client and herself. She explains feeling taken back from the start; the client's age, way of walking and talking made her feel 'very young'. Dan's presented problem was panic attacks, but Aida explores how his behaviour contradicted his words.

'I think it was a mixture of him projecting an image of himself as self-sufficient at all cost, and me being caught up in my fears of not being good enough.' concludes Aida.

## Reflection

The case study with Aida highlights the difference between talking about and enacting events and emotions. Gilbert and Evans encourage the supervisee to regard supervision as a place where s/he 'is offered the safe space in which to feel his feeling unedited' (2000: 11). Does this reflect your own experience of supervision so far?

The supervisor can help with reframing problems with, for instance, the supervisee's own internalised object relations in mind, but it is a matter of co-constructing links rather than 'teaching facts' to the supervisee. The term 'parallel process' is often, as suggested, used in psychoanalytically inspired therapy to address how material outside our direct awareness at the time, i.e., 'unconscious' material, imposes on the therapeutic relationship. The most common form of parallel process happens when the therapists bring their 'story' about their clients through enactments rather than with words. It is often something that the therapist is unaware of but offers a clue for the supervisor through changes in behaviour. Page and Wasket write:

> Most supervisors welcome such parallel phenomena as the resulting dynamic provide a more direct way of experiencing the counselling process than second-hand reporting by the counsellor ... An example of this would be a counsellor who, when working with a particularly passive client, starts to act in an atypical passive manner towards his supervisor. Thus the passivity within the client–counsellor relationship is paralleled in the counsellor–supervisor relationship. (Page & Wasket, 2006: 113)

The parallel process can, however, also go the other way; experiences from the therapist–supervisor relationship can become enacted in the client–therapist relationship. If, for instance, the supervisor is uninterested or overly critical in ways which the therapist feel unable to address or acknowledge, there is a risk that the therapist brings this material into the client relationship. Page and Wosket continue:

> [I]t is equally possible for supervisory dynamics to be reflected in the counselling relationship. An example of this is when the supervisor acts in a rather punitive and critical manner towards his supervisee, who in turn acts in a similar manner towards the client. (Page & Wosket, 2006: 113)

With the risks for parallel processes in mind, Frawley-O'Dea and Sarnat stress the importance of addressing a need 'know it all' if it appears to be there. Like therapists, supervisors can be under a cultural pressure to 'know' and deal with a 'powerful cultural pressure to feel like competent, objective experts in order to acknowledge their ... responses' (Frawley-O'Dea & Sarnat, 2001: 122). This is something which Adams (2014) resonates with in her study, addressing a common need for collusion.

## How can you monitor the relationships?

Without a shared understanding it is difficult to monitor how the relationship is progressing.

Making notes after each supervision session can help you to keep track both with regard to separate session and with regard to development over time. It is perhaps helpful to make a note of your own feelings and reactions in supervision and discuss the supervisory relationship with your supervisor.

It is good practice for supervisors to contract with supervisees such that both parties know how they will work together including how and when they will review their work together and any practical details needed. It might also help to monitor the supervisory relationship in terms thinking about how it meets your ethical, educational and personal needs. Inskipp and Proctor (2001) suggest we think of supervision as addressing normative, formative and restorative needs:

- Your **normative needs** could include concerns or issues connected with professional and ethical guidelines, norms and laws. For example, does supervision help you to examine the ethical requirement of being 'trustworthy'?; do you feel supported enough to monitor the process of keeping your word to your clients and do what you say you will do?
- Your **formative needs** involve skills, theoretical knowledge and personal attributes as a practitioner. Do you feel supported in providing a service 'working within your competence'? Do you feel safe enough to explore your personal and professional limitations, including talking about obstacles for not finding it easy to do so? Is it OK to be 'wrong'?

'Self-care' is equally important and the Ethical Framework commits us to 'ensuring that our well-being is sufficient to sustain the quality of work'. Continuing professional development and research are essential requirements for practice. Will your supervisor, for instance, help you to develop skills in reading, discussing and maybe undertaking research?

- Your **restorative needs** revolve around being supported and sometimes constructively challenged with regard to how your personal issues or prejudices may affect your work with clients. Self-care is an essential aspect being 'trustworthy' and of 'self-respect' (Ethical Framework principles) in your practice. Hawkins and Shohet (2005) compare the supervisory relationship with a 'nursing triad', where the supervisor helps the supervisee to 'hold' the client. They remind us of the psychoanalyst Donald Winnicott who coined the concept of being 'good enough' and asserted that 'it is hard to be "good enough" unless [being] held and supported'(Winnicott cited in Hawkins and Shohet, 2005: 83).

## Potential problems

We saw earlier how we may prevent ourselves from taking space, being heard and supported – suggesting that 'supervision is only as good as we allow it to be' (Adams, 2014: 177). Research about supervisory relationship (Carroll & Gilbert, 2005) addresses, however, at least three common areas of conflict, namely

**Differences in theoretical orientation.** Although supervision involves learning from new perspectives, theoretical differences can lead to both confusion and disagreement. As suggested earlier, the sooner you address differences and overlaps with regard to theory and underpinning philosophy, for instance with regard to the therapeutic relationship and the role of the therapist, the better.

**Style of supervision.** Sometimes there is confusion around 'style', for instance with regard to how formal or informal supervision should be. Supervision is not therapy, but we are not 'reporting back' to a boss or a manager either. It is something in between. This can, as suggested, be a dual process – where collusion around both being 'good' and 'right' need to be attended to.

**Self-care.** The British Association for Counselling and Psychotherapy (BACP, 2018) ethical guidelines below are usually considered carefully by counsellors and psychotherapists with regard to their clients and their needs. But good practice requires that therapists also apply the guidelines to themselves. Do you do that?

## Activity 3.3

### To what extent do you meet the guidelines?

- **Fidelity**. Am I being true to myself? Do I really want to see this client? Is it right for me, my family and friends, to take on this client at this stage? Do I need more time for myself?
- **Autonomy**. Am I considering all factors in my own life when I take on this case? Am I making an informed decision with regard to my own needs and interests right now? Do I 'know' what I am doing, right now, with my own needs in mind?
- **Beneficence**. Where are my own interests in all this? Is this choice serving my own best interests? Am I considering both the short- and long-term effects on myself – for instance, psychical and emotional effects?
- **Non-maleficence**. Am I possibly doing myself harm with my decision to take on a new client, to work evenings or to continue working in general?
- **Justice**. What price might I be paying to help others? Am I doing myself justice? Am I fair to myself? If not, why? And what do I need to find a comfortable balance?

After this exercise, take some time to return to the here and now. Allow yourself to leave your own practice behind and immerse yourself in the case study below when you feel ready.

Reflective, good practice is complex and involves listening inwards and outwardly at the same time as considering theoretical and practical frameworks. A reflective therapist tends to ask him- or herself:

- What is the client communicating verbally and non-verbally?
- What am I 'hearing' and how?
- What do I feel?
- What do I think? How do I structure and frame the information that I receive? Where does my understanding of the present situation come from? Could I frame my understanding in any other way?
- **Consider either a recurring, or isolated, powerful event which has impacted you lately. Once you have decided on a problem, approach it with the ACCTT stages below.**

## Phase 1: Acknowledging a problem: listening to the 'rattling noise' of your engine

Personal development typically focuses on learning more about the 'engine that drives us'. Consider a critical event as you experienced it, list what comes to your mind regarding

a. What happened, and
b. What comes up when re-connecting with your embodied responses to that experience.

Recalling feeling drained, hollow, angry, shamed or agitated may be some of the responses. Maybe feeling 'wired' as in the earlier case example with Helen in her supervision? Or feeling overly gushing and active? This stage of transformative learning revolves around 'leaning into' your often intuitive responses, to stay and explore rather than avoid, escape or maybe displace, enact them.

### Case study 3.3

**Drawing on intuitive responses**

Joanne returns home after a session with Alicia, a long-term client. She closes her eyes and remains still for a while to easier re-connect with the experience. She then jots down some thoughts: 'Jet lagged', she writes. 'I feel exhausted and empty after the session.'

Tracing the opening verbatim from memory, she notices how much she must have been talking about the weather and other insignificant things to fill the space. She tries to reconnect with their meeting by writing in dialogue:

| | |
|---|---|
| Alicia: | Hello, how are you? |
| Joanne: | I'm fine, thanks, and you? |
| Alicia (sighs): | Oh, alright I suppose. Okay weather at least. |
| Joanne: | Yes, lovely. It seems to have improved, more sun now ... |

## Phase 2: Considering the situation

Considering the situation on a 'unistructural' level involves considering the problem as we do when first hearing a 'rattling' sound in the 'engine'. Is it at all familiar? How serious might it be? Turning the attention to you, you might consider it in context of earlier situations. How does that kind of event 'sit' in the context of your own history, personally and/or professionally? Have you ever experienced something like this before? What does it make you feel like, and have you *felt* like that before? If so, when? What does the event(s) share with previous events? These questions will typically require an environment where it feels safe for you to 'sit with' what is going on, maybe to associate freely and brainstorm. We need someone who we feel is on our side, at this stage a supervisor in the first place, or a critical friend who can see where you are coming from and will respect how you feel but also help you to bring in a new and different perspective.

### Case study 3.4

#### Considering 'jet lag' further, in free writing

To continue to prepare to speak with her supervisor, Joanne probes further into her relationship with Alicia through 'free writing'. She writes without stopping:

> I feel 'jet lagged', exhausted and empty after the session ... I've given everything I've got. What more can I give ... What more do you want ... when will you ever listen to me ...

As she writes, Joanne notices how she begins to write with her father in mind. The busy, strict, demanding father – who Joanne adapted to by always being charming, witty and light.

## Phase 3: Connecting

'Connecting' symbolises in the context of the ACCTT model moving from a uni- to a multistructural perspective to view the issue into a larger context. This includes trying to conceptualise your strong response to your client from different perspectives:

*You and your theory*

- How can, firstly, your reaction be explained and discussed within your own modality? Consider the event and your relationship in the context of a theory. Countertransference is described as a frequently used term to explore therapists' response. How might that concept help – or not help – you?

- The issue of modality can be considered in the context of Schön's suggestion about the often occurring 'gap' between our espoused theory and an
  actual theory in action. How – if at all – might that come into play in your
  practice when put under pressure? **What might you need to help you
  decrease that gap? More personal support? More professional support? More training? How does your work setting suit you and the
  way you work?** If, for instance, you work in short-term settings, might
  you improve your knowledge about referral options? Are there transdisciplinary opportunities where you work, where different theories could be
  integrated?
- The 'considering stage' also involves positioning the problem in context of
  other modalities. Expanding your reading into other therapeutic theories
  can be particularly significant.
- Can you undertake more training if you sense that your practice might
  benefit from a theoretical breadth? Can you discuss theoretical breadth
  with your supervisor?
- Personal and professional development play a key role in the ACCTT
  model, especially from this phase onwards. And ongoing engagement
  in further discussions, reading, own writing, CPD and engaging different types and stages of research are paramount aspects of reflective
  practice.

## Activity 3.4   Comparing your theory through a literature review

A literature review summarises and synthesises academic research on chosen topics. It involves exploring your question and interest in terms of experiences, definitions and findings made by other practitioner-researchers in the field. Your literature review will typically include

- A summary of existing work, including ways in which your topic has been studied and the issues and outcomes from those studies.
- A critical evaluation of those works, for instance with attention to the methods and methodologies.
- Conclusions about the studies and work done to date in your field, both for the sake of evidencing the history of the topic and to justify your own planned study.

Your own approach will be positioned in other theories and approaches.

Although access to a university library certainly helps, the EBSCO platform with access to PsycINFO, PsycARTICLES and Psychology & Behavioral Sciences Collection (PBSC) are some good starting points. Electronic sources are increasingly

*(Continued)*

emphasised, and some member organisations – like the BACP – offer its members access to platforms like EBSCO. The inclusion and exclusion criteria will be specific to your search and are important to take note of. The 'trying out' of different search words and phrases usually helps to tighten up the research question: emphasis, focus, line of enquiry and outcome may surprise and lead into new or different search paths – which is all part of the literature review. Online search facilities like Research Gate and Google Scholar offer open access to existing research on different topics.

Experiment with some different 'search words': what captures your interest? What kind of responses come up? What are the findings – and how were those findings reached?

**Doing a literature review might seem daunting. If it does, please either wait or to go to Activity 5.2 on p. 78 (Keeping up-to-date with research) to do this exercise.**

*Social positioning*

How might, secondly, your responses and strategies be viewed in context of different social positions, for instance in relation to class, gender and culture? This question is often difficult to explore since 'the last one to see the water is the fish', as the old proverb suggests. Alvesson and Skoldeberg (2000) suggest adopting a reflexive 'ironic deconstruction', where you 'defamiliarise' yourself as a way of engaging with another perspective for long enough to see your old one from a new perspective. One option is to, for instance, view the traditional use of transference through the lens of 'cultural countertransference' (Eleftheriadou, 2010). We will return to this later on. At this stage, the point is to consider how reflective practice involves 'transformative learning', as the earlier mentioned Mezirow (2009) coined the phrase when considering how an openness and interest in 'engaging in disorienting dilemmas' invariably challenge our current beliefs about the world, so that problematic frames of reference lead to more inclusive, open, and 'emotionally able to change' frames (Mezirow, 2009: 18). An important aspect of reflective practice is in this sense an openness to critically appreciate one's own theory of practice through a dialectical engagement with other practices.

## Case Study 3.5

### Connecting on a 'multistructural' level

The post-structural philosopher Michel Foucault explores implicit and explicit power in medical assessment over time, for instance, with regard to the historical development of 'hysteria'. Foucault's texts on *Madness and Civilisation* throw a chilling light on to therapeutic practice, as he expands on the theme of mental health 'care':

It is thought that Tuke and Pinel opened the asylum to medical knowledge. They did not introduce science, but a personality, whose powers borrowed from science only their disguise, or at most their justification. These powers, by their nature, were of a moral and social order ...

Pinel cites the case of a girl of seventeen who had been raised by her parents with 'extreme indulgence'; she had fallen into a 'giddy, mad delirium without any cause that could be determined'; at the hospital she was treated with great gentleness, but she always showed a certain 'haughtiness' which could not be tolerated at the asylum; she spoke 'of her parents with nothing but bitterness'.

It was decided to subject her to a regime of strict authority; the keeper, 'in order to tame this inflexible character, seized the moment of the bath and expressed himself forcibly concerning certain unnatural persons who dared oppose their parents and disdain their authority ... she was henceforth soothed and could not sufficiently express her gratitude toward the keeper who had brought an end to her continual agitation, and had restored tranquillity and calmed her heart'. (Foucault, 1984: 160–61).

Foucault's criticism of psychotherapy as a conveyor of values and beliefs about right and wrong, sane and insane, etc. under 'the pretence of being science', is a disturbing one to most therapists. Tuke and Pinel act on a moral and social order, writes Foucault, and he highlights through this the importance of considering the dyad of therapist and client in the context of time and place. Power within the mental health sector is often 'inherent'; it is rarely explicit or easy to spot. Psychotherapy is always part of a bigger, social system. What role might we, as therapists, play today in preserving gender, class or culturally-specific roles and expectations? And what can we learn from other practices, to integrate new theories into our existing ones?

Consider *your* practice as if looking back 30 years from now. What signifies our society in terms of values and beliefs about self and others? What stands out as good, bad, normal and not normal? How might these values influence our role as therapists today? What might be viewed critically by someone considering our therapeutic practice from a not-too-distant future?

## Phase 4: Transforming the experience into practice, first stage

This stage of your reflection involves putting your new learning into practice in the context of your modality. It does not necessarily mean 'doing' new things but is likely to impact the way that you relate to your client. You may notice problems with your own resistance in mind, or in the context of what our modality informs you in terms of relational stances and means of putting that into concepts and theory. Observe what helps you grow and feel supported, in terms of peers, supervision, work–life balance and CPD.

## Phase 5: Transforming on an extended abstract level, second stage

During this phase you will typically generalise about the problem, for instance through comparing it to other situations and transfer principles and ideas underlying this specific instance onto other contexts. The previous 'connection' and 'transformative learning' stage (Phase 1) are likely to have included new learning from other modalities and new theories. This phase signifies a meta-perspective, where a new sense of seeing parts in relation to the whole may emerge. The original problem has now triggered a chain of new insights, which hopefully will affect the way you approach our role as therapist with new curiosity, as in the case study below with the therapist Foziha Hamid who experienced a problem in her clinical practice which she turned into research.

### Case study 3.6   Transforming practice stage 2

#### Example: Doing research

Foziha works as an integrative psychotherapist, supervisor and clinical manager against sexual and domestic violence at the Women and Girls Network (WGN). Foziha felt overwhelmed in her practice in relation to how an increasing use of technology across all aspects of individual lives have impacted the use of the internet for sexual behaviours. She experienced a sense of helplessness and her own burnout. Turning her attention to others, she noticed other therapists reporting feeling ill-prepared to work with newly presented problems linked to trolling, revenge pornography, trafficking, availability of pornography online and theories about rape culture. When seeking information in ongoing research through a literature search, she found very little. Her sense of absence of language for women to explore and talk about sexual victimisation online triggered an interest into narrative research focusing on how stories both convey and produce narratives about self and others. She decided to research how to improve practice with clients sexually victimised by the use of technology, drawing from narrative research. She decided in turn to explore practitioners' ways of constructing meaning in relation to technology-facilitated sexual violence against adult women. She interviewed advice workers, psychotherapists and counsellors about how they work in relation to the issue and explore what impact this has in their practice. The study lead to themes which helped Foziha to develop training to transform practice within and beyond her own agency.

## Reflection

Transforming on an 'extended abstract level' might, as suggested, result in undertaking research. We will return to that at different stages of this book.

- What might you benefit from learning more about? Have you got a plan for further training?
- What is your relationship to research? Take some time to consider yourself in relation to research.
- Are you already involved in research? If not, what has prevented you so far from approaching research?
- Using one word to describe what you think about research, what would you chose? Keep it, to return to it at the end of this book.

# 4

# Reflecting on relationships

## Core knowledge

Psychotherapy shares with reflective practice its interest in our subjective understanding of self and others.

- We will look at concepts like 'locus of evaluation', 'automatic thoughts' and 'transference' to explore psychotherapeutic framings for reflections on self in relation to others.
- We will consider the concept 'countertransference' among other concepts, to reflect specifically on the therapists' emotions and use of self.

## Reflecting on relatedness and feelings

There is much written about how to draw on the therapeutic relationship to support the client's reflection on her/his ways of relating to the world.

There is less said about the therapists' opportunities to reflect on experiences, decision makings and actions with past and present relationships in mind.

The client's relationships to the therapists was in the original psychoanalysis understood to 'be unconsciously influenced, coloured and distorted by earlier childhood experiences' (Holmes & Lindley, 1998: 126). Freud developed a theory about an 'ambivalent transference' (1959: 38) which 'comprises positive and affectionate as well as negative and hostile attitudes towards the analyst'. Freud writes:

> The patient sees in his analyst the return – the reincarnation – of some important figure out of his childhood or past, and consequently transfers on to him feelings and reactions that undoubtedly applied to this model. (Freud, 1959: 38)

Freud considered the lived experience as a crucial aspect of the talking cure, asserting that 'the patient never forgets again what he has experienced in the form of transference' (Freud, 1959: 41).

The relationship was reflected upon with an interest in what the client might project and 'put' onto the therapists, the therapists' relational experiences were guided by a focus on how the client might re-enact their childhood experiences in the room.

## Countertransference

The original Freudian one-person perspective assumed in this sense an expert-driven 'doing to' stance, where the therapist's response was conceptualised in terms of countertransference that described a reaction to something which inevitably was 'owned' (and misplaced) by the client's defences and projections. One of the earliest and most lasting concepts for therapists' emotional, embodied responses in the therapeutic relationship has been 'countertransference'. Jung was a forerunner in expanding the concept of countertransference, suggesting that for projections to really latch on there needs to be a hook in carrier; a projection will, in other words, hook on to a therapist for a special reason. Racker (2001: 133) resonated with the view of therapy as a fusion of past and the present for both therapists and clients. Racker distinguished, for instance, between concordant and complementary countertransference, which the integrative therapist Clarkson later developed in terms of 'reactive' and 'proactive' countertransference (Clarkson, 2002: 9). With nuances within each term, Clarkson reserved the first category for responses originating in the client:

- Reactive countertransference describes the psychotherapist's feelings that are elicited by or induced by the patient.
- Proactive countertransference refers to feelings, atmospheres, projections, etc. that can be said to have been introduced by the psychotherapist themselves.

The broadened, pluralistic approach (Valerio, 2017) to countertransference assumes that both therapists' and clients' meaning-making processes and subjective understanding of the world is firstly changeable and ongoingly influenced by other experiences. Rowan and Jacobs (2003) suggest that 'countertransference has generally been underestimated by humanistic therapists' (Rowan & Jacobs, 2003: 22). Valerio (2017) offers a broad range of approaches across modalities to countertransference. In the account below, the CBT therapist Devon (2017) explores, for instance, how 'emotions, physical changes and behaviours' can be explored through a countertransference lens also in Cognitive Behavioural Therapy (p. 90). Despite transference not being a 'central tool' in CBT, 'automatic thoughts and emotions related to the dynamics of the therapeutic relationship' is increasingly regarded as a valuable learning opportunity to modify behaviour, writes Devon; and countertransference is helpful to explore and reflect on 'automatic thoughts and schemata in the clinician' (Devon, 2017: 91). Devon stresses also how 'an intellectual understanding ... does not stop the unconscious processes in the room and hence the importance of some understanding of the unconscious and one's own therapy for all practitioners' (p. 91). An intellectual understanding continues with an example with 'Sue':

> In my first session with Sue, she said she was always disappointed by people. They always let her down and she became really angry and hurt. She gave me examples ... From a CBT perspective, her core beliefs were about being unlovable ... As she told me more of her previous experiences of people letting her down and the rage she felt, I felt highly anxious and stressed. I was aware of my heart pounding; I was tense and felt hot ... We worked on her negative automatic thoughts and behaviours. She came late to the next sessions and I was aware that I was relieved ... On reflection, my own core belief about feeling not good enough and the desire to please others had led to my anxiety about knowing that I would displease Sue ... My core beliefs of not being likeable and a fear of being abandoned are combined with a conditional assumption that if I try really hard I can please people ... I had not used my feeling to deal with the therapy-interfering behaviours which could have helped us to deal more effectively with her (and my) unconscious processes. (Devon, 2017: 91)

There are now multiple approaches to countertransference. Rowan and Jacobs (2003) refer to seven types. They highlight, however, how 'counter' can be approached as either 'against' or 'alongside', depending on the therapists' understanding of their role in terms of being about 'doing to' or 'being with' in therapy.

## Activity 4.1

In the case study below, the therapists Joanne reflects over her emotional response to her client Alicia. Please read it with the distinction between 'reactive' and 'proactive' countertransference in mind. How might you have planned the process with Alicia?

## Case study 4.1

### Joanne and Alicia 1

Joanne practices as honorary (placement) psychotherapist in a psychodynamic therapy service within the NHS. The service provides free long-term psychotherapy on a weekly basis for a maximum of 2 years. Alicia, 45, seeks therapy in the aftermath of a traffic accident. She is a large woman, looks slightly unkempt and sits down with a deep sigh. She remains looking at a spot on the wall behind the therapist (Joanne) whilst describing how she has not felt able to leave home after a car ran into hers at a traffic light. Alicia is divorced since 8 years ago, with no children, and is unemployed after selling the company she shared with her husband. She seems docile, admitting to 'taking anti-depressants' which makes her 'sleep much'. The therapists register with interest a sense of disengagement, as if Alicia feels 'too much' and she would have preferred her to leave the room. She wonders if this might be how Alicia's mother felt, with Alicia as her last child in what Alicia has described as a trouble-some marriage. Is this how Alicia got used to being seen and experienced? Did this become a blueprint? The sequence of the traffic event – as a sudden, unjust and unpredictable attack – seems to repeat itself. There is a sense of hopelessness as a starting point from all Alicia's experiences. Joanne notices a sense of disconnection; the pull to disconnect makes her smile, nod and talk more than she would in other sessions. She also watches the session go over the time.

In the example, Joanne is trained to listen out for her own strong emotional reactions in response to her clients, and she tends to understand that in context of 'countertransference'. How do you consider your responses in the context of your own modality? How does that help you to understand the therapeutic relationship?

---

The case study with Alicia and Joanne continues below, four months later. Joanne has explored her strong want to detach herself from Alicia, together with an almost irresistible pull to talk, smile and allow sessions to go over time. Her supervisor helped her to explore this strong, slightly overwhelming response in the context of her history of finding her sense of self-worth through being charming, light and facilitating. She discusses how she has found Alicia's needs overwhelming, as if an underlying disappointment was there from the start. Her own response to looming disappointments is often to please, charm and bring light. This feels repeated now. Alicia and her therapist Joanne have now worked together for 14 weeks, within their long-term contract of two years within the psychodynamic long-term service within the NHS.

---

## Case study 4.2

### Alicia and Joanne 2

Alicia has reduced her intake of anti-depressants and often engages well in the sessions. She has explored her traffic accident in the context of her feelings around it, which during one session she referred to as 'helpless, hopeless,

*(Continued)*

totally powerless and paralyzingly terrified'. To the Joannes' question about if she ever had felt like that before, she cried and described an incident when working as a baby-sitter for their next-door neighbours, the father of the child raped her. Alicia was 13 years old. She never told anyone about it. In another session, she explored helplessness, hopelessness and powerlessness in context of her family. As the youngest child of three, by parents bound by an unhappy relationship, Alicia got used to avoiding adding to her parents' troubles. She would struggle to recall any memories at all of closeness and explored the rape by the neighbour in the context of having grown used to coping on her own. Therapist Joanne has, in turn, felt able to explore in supervision her need to offer gushing charm in tense interactions, having re-connected with where the 'need' originated from and belonged. She has felt able to finish sessions on time and to allow for silences when appropriate as her modality privileges.

Today is Alicia's and Joanne's 15th session. Alicia arrives slightly flushed in her cheeks, in a colourful dress with big flowers. Alicia has so far worn brown and grey, mostly a well-worn brown pullover with a grey striped jersey skirt.

Alicia:     Hi there!

Joanne:     (Silence. Joanne's reflection-in-action suggests waiting to respond to avoid impacting the relationship before Alicia does. Alicia has got a new dress, which might bring something about progress – but just as well not. Joanne's reflection-in-action suggests waiting to see what unravels, to potentially learn more about these responses before she says anything. Her chosen action is to remain silent.)

Alicia:     It's my birthday today.

Joanne:     (Again, remaining silent fits well within the therapist's modality – but this is an unusual event, and Joanne has to reflect-in-action and make an on-the-spot experiment based on an embodied sense of tension in the room. She gets the sense of a girl-like smile when Alicia tilts her head and smiles, and she considers an incongruence between Alicia's smile and what they have talked about earlier. Joanne's reflection-in-action suggests waiting to see what unravels, to potentially learn more about these responses before she says anything.)

Alicia:     I might treat myself to a present.

Joanne:     (Continued silence. Her reflection-in-action suggests that she will hear from Alicia about what might be underneath the smile.)

Alicia:     Or I might go home and go to bed. What do you care?

Joanne:     (Silent.)

Alicia:     I even kicked the dog today, I felt like tying him outside in the garden last night – to the big, lurking foxes …

Joanne:     (Remains silent. She notices feeling overwhelmed, as if Alicia is very big and difficult to like. The verbal attack on the dog makes Joanne slightly dizzy – her reflection-in-action tells her that she has felt like this before, when Alicia moves quickly between victim to perpetrator mood without showing compassion for the victim while seeming helpless and wanting support herself. Joanne's reflection-in-action suggests that this makes sense in context of Alicia's background. Some of her feelings seems to fit the responses of Alicia's mother, who Alicia describes as seeming exasperated; as if Alicia always was too much, that this is some of what might have been underneath Alicia's earlier responses. Jumping in too early with a 'congratulations, nice dress' might have prevented this from surfacing. Joanne's reflection-in-action suggests that this moment lends itself to address that.) ... It sounds like you are wondering if I care for you?

Alicia:    Yes, I was thinking this morning, why should Joanne care? Alicia, you're a fool to think she'll be the slightest bothered about your new dress. She's only here for her salary, birthdays or new dresses or not. I was really looking forward to coming, I'm looking forward to coming more and more ...

Joanne:    (Silent. Joanne is watching Alicia, who's looking out if the window as she speaks, as if lost in thought.)

Alicia:    ... and that feels weird ...

Joanne:    I'm glad that you come here ...

Alicia:    (Crying, but now smiling between tears.) Part of me hates you, you know! It goes against my principles to trust, you know that.

Joanne:    ... part of you hates me ...

Alicia:    ... yes, it feels so scary ...

Joanne:    (Remains silent. The silence seems warm, as if filling the room. Joanne's embodied response to Alicia is sensing warmth and intense affection. Joanne looks at Alicia, who turns towards Joanne and meets her eyes. They hold each other gaze for a long time, both smiling.)

Alicia begins to talk about memories of her mother often travelling, leaving home to stay with friends and relatives, without bringing Alicia along. She starts remembering one birthday in particular ...

---

## Reflection

Joanne is trained to adopt a relational focus, where she considers her embodied responses. Being silent in order to not preempt opportunities for the client to connect with negative emotions is significant within her psychodynamic perspective. How does your modality help or not help you to work with your responses in mind?

   Discuss (if possible in pairs) how you would have responded to Alicia about her birthday, and why.

Humanistic therapy asserts that 'there is no compelling reason to assume that 'fundamental' (that is, important, basic) and 'first' (that is, chronologically first) are identical concepts' (Yalom, 1980: 11). The therapeutic process involves tapping into something which already is there 'implicit, but unverbalised' in most clients, and one of the overriding goals with therapy, suggests Rogers (1961), is 'the dawning realization that [we] can base a value judgement supplied by [our] own senses [and] own experiences' (p. 150). To facilitate this Rogers (1961: 35) says that the 'rational of the counselor's role [is about] entering the world' of the client 'as completely as I am able' to share the client's 'experiencing' (p. 35) so that the s/he 'can examine various aspects of his experience as they ... are apprehended through his sensory and visceral equipment, without distorting them to fit the existing concept of self' (p. 76).

Rogers uses the term 'locus of evaluation' to understand difficulties when we 'evaluate' our experiences. Rogers (1961) observed a common 'tendency for the locus of evaluation to lie outside' the person: 'In therapy, in the initial phases, there appears to be a tendency for the locus of evaluation to lie outside the client. It is seen as a function of parents, of the culture, of friends, and of the counsellor' (p. 51). Rogers (1961) writes: 'in client-centred therapy ... one description of the counsellor's behaviour is that he consistently keeps the locus of evaluation with the client' (p. 151). This involves in turn striving to achieve someone's 'frame of references [with] the expressed ideas and attitudes from the other person's point of view [and to] "sense how it feels to him"' (Rogers, 1961: 332), so that the client 'in the absence of any actual or implied threats to self' allows him or herself to 'examine various aspects of his experience as they ... are apprehended through his sensory and visceral equipment, without distorting them to fit the existing concept of self (p. 76).

Buber (1947/1971) and Rogers and both wrote about the impact of moments when 'deep realness in one meets a realness in the other' (Rogers, 1961: 151). Rogers refers to the therapeutic relationship as a place for phenomenological understanding guided by attempts to 'reciprocal experience' (1961: 26).

## Activity 4.2   Active listening

You will remember the listening exercise from Chapter 1. You need a partner for this exercise, which focuses on active listening. Please remind yourselves about how to prepare for the exercise. This time you will be invited to be more active, in the way that Rogers referred to as the 'rational' for counselling in terms of 'achieving someone's frame of references [with] the expressed ideas and attitudes from the *other person's point of view* [to] sense how it feels to him' (Rogers, 1961: 332; emphasis added). Existential therapists refer to this aim in terms of 'entering' and sharing the client's 'phenomenology [or] experiential world' (Yalom, 1980: 17). The existentialist philosopher Merleau-Ponty draws our attention to how in the experience of dialogue, there is … a common ground … a dual being, where the other is for me no longer a mere bit of behaviour in my transcendental field, nor I in his. Our perspectives merge into each other, and we exist through a common world. (Merleau-Ponty, 1999: 200)

Rowan and Jacobs refer to this level of deep empathic attunement as a 'second level of empathy' characterised by an aim to be 'in their shoes, seeing through their eyes, but at the same time retaining one's own identity' (Rowan & Jacobs, 2003: 47).

## To the one speaking

Talk about a personal subject for ten minutes.

## To the one listening

Listen with the view of 'standing in the other's shoes' or seeing 'through his/her eyes' whilst retaining your own identity, as Rowan and Jacobs suggest.

## Afterwards

Revisit the earlier checklist to explore what might have come up for each of you, as you speak and as you listen. Compare the experience of listening in this way. You may both want to make notes about difficulties as well as positives involved in this kind of listening. Make notes of whom – if at all – you feel you can turn to, to explore this in a supportive way.

This 'intentional understanding' guided by 'deep hearing' aims to hear with rather than about the other. It has been explored in other contexts, in terms of, for instance, what Habermas (1987) refers to as a 'communicative rationality', where the aim of the interaction is about understanding each others' viewpoints instead of proving one's own point, which tends to be the dominating 'rationality' behind human interaction in a society guided by a 'technical rationality'. It is a dialectic, transformative process that inevitably influences both parties through the nature of immersion of new and other frameworks. Rogers' (1995) refers to these moments as 'memorable I–Thou relationships'; he suggests that these 'deep and mutual personal encounters does not happen often, but I am convinced that unless it happens occasionally, we are not living as human beings' (Rogers, 1995: 8). We referred earlier to Mearns and Cooper's (2018) developed relational theory based on humanistic principles. They draw from the term 'relational depth' to describe 'state of profound contact and engagement between two people in which each person is fully real with the Other, and able to understand and value the Other's experiences at a high level'. Finlay (2016) describes relational therapy as an umbrella term for approaches offering a 'micro-cosm' of the social world, so that what happens in the therapy room can reflect processes happening outside – and vice versa. The significance of 'between' brings focus on an intersubjective space between where 'we touch and are touched by the Other in multiple, often unseen ways'. The therapist is present – and there to explore and share upcoming relational experiences. The relationship works as a collaborative partnership. Both parties contribute to the relationship so that therapy becomes a joint enterprise. This resonates in turn with Schön's idea of a reflective contract around a 'virtual world'.

## Reflective contract

The emphasis on a reciprocal, jointly felt understanding underpins Schön's term 'reflective contract' (Table 4.1). Schön emphasises, as mentioned earlier, the significance of 'the practitioner's reflective conversation with a situation' and how this rests on the sense that s/he makes 'of the situation must include his own contribution to it' (Schön, 1983: 163). He speaks about aiming to 'step into the client's shoes', which is often focused on in the emphasis on intersubjectivity expressed in both humanistic and psychoanalytic theory. He refers to a 'reflective contract' where the therapist 'becomes adept at his relationship with the [client] into a world of inquiry in which thoughts and feeling can be seen as sources of discovery rather than as triggers to action' (Schön, 1983: 161). The contract depends, in turn, on the therapist's

> ability to empathize, to establish and honour trust guided by the norms of their mutual obligations, reflect on their own experience of being with the client with an interest in signs of countertransference responses, and to help the client 'gain insight from revealed thought and feeling so that the efforts of the special relationship comes to seem worthwhile'. (Schön, 1983: 161)

Schön refers to this process as a 'virtual world', which becomes 'both a method of inquiry and a strategy of intervention'. Schön sees in this sense 'action-present' stages in therapeutic practice where 'iterations and variations of actions [to] be tried' within a reflective contract where the practitioner always becomes part of the process (1983: 161). The therapeutic relationship becomes a 'virtual world' that works as 'contexts for experiments' (Schön, 1983: 129). The idea of reflecting over ones' own shaping of situations is fundamental to this. Schön suggests that in 'reflective conversations', the practitioner approaches each situation as an *'experient'*. The 'reflective practitioner' balances ideally uncertainty with the 'curiosity of a child', and explores situations 'as if for the first time' The 'sense he makes of it must, as mentioned, include his own contribution to it' (Schön, 1983: 163) within a 'reflective contract' (Table 4.1) allowing for practitioner's own uncertainty and openness to be welcomed into the process.

*Table 4.1* Schön's reflective contract

| Expert | Reflective practitioner |
|---|---|
| I am presumed to know, and must claim to do so, regardless of my own uncertainty. | I am presumed to know, but I am not the only one in the situation to have relevant and important knowledge. My uncertainties may be a source of learning for me and for them. |
| Keep my distance from the client and hold on to the expert's role. Give the client a sense of my expertise but convey a feeling of warmth and sympathy as a 'sweetener'. | Seek out connections to the client's thoughts and feelings. Allow his respect for my knowledge to emerge from his discovery of it in the situation. |
| Look for deference and status in the client's response to my professional persona. | Look for the sense of freedom and of real connection to the client, as a consequence of no longer needing to maintain a professional façade. |

*Source*: Schön (1983: 300). Republished with permission of the Hachette Books Group; permission conveyed through Copyright Clearance Center, Inc.

Different modalities offer different frameworks to reflect over our emotions as part of our the on-the-spot experimenting at the junction of out-of-awareness responses and decision makings and actions as therapists. Many therapists will, as McLeod and Balamoutsou, 'consistently use language permeated by feelings' (2001: 142):

- the **central significance of feeling**, for instance: 'so when you're starting a fight you are actually feeling really scared ...'
- the **existence of an inner world**, like: 'so, are you saying that on the outside you're always happy, but inside you're actually feeling ...'
- a self **comprised of 'parts'**, like: 'it's like a part of you still is very angry ...'
- the value of **experiencing what is felt here and now**, for instance: 'You looked tearful, right then ... when you're talking about the dinner with your family. Can we perhaps try to stay with that feeling that came up, could you try to tell me what you're feeling right now ...'

## The messiness of being human

Psychological 'realities' are likely to fall within a category which we typically refer to as 'messy' in the sense that they are ambivalent and changing – and as practitioners we tend to direct our focus on 'truth', which often as Symington suggests 'cannot be measured but it does exist':

> Most psychological realities do not have the property of extension or tangibility; a dream, a hallucination, a belief, a thought. Truth is a reality of this nature. It cannot be measured but it does exist; the fact that is it difficult to define does not detract from this. (Symington, 1986: 17)

## The therapists' emotional world

In the case study below, Lisa Champion shares her experiences from seeking ways of reflecting on therapists' own use of emotions in therapy. Lisa describes her journey into a 'phenomenological enquiry into the therapists' emotional world'. You are encouraged to read it with your own emotions in mind: how do you reflect over your emotional world? At the end of it, Lisa shares a reflective writing exercise, which she has used when learning to 'write phenomenologically'.

### Case study 4.3

#### Reflecting on your emotional world as a therapist, by Lisa Champion, PhD candidate at Metanoia

I am a budding doctoral student, drawn into the world of research because of my interest in the emotional world of psychotherapists. Both the theory that underpinned my work and on what I was noticing about myself as I was working with my clients, has been a major catalyst for my interest. The reflection on theory started with my training in emotionally focused theory, which suggests that the client's emotional 'way of being' in the world influences their well-being and their relationship to themselves and others. This theoretical framework has had a strong influence on my clinical work, but I was surprised how little attention was being paid to the therapists' emotional way of being.

Early in my career, I noticed feelings that I was having when I was working; I felt, for instance, an energy vibrating within me that made me sit up straighter, talk faster and start 'working too hard'. Sometimes, especially when I didn't know the answer to something or felt confused, I noticed a tightness in my chest and a sense of a protective barrier rising up around me. These feelings were far from what I wanted to experience when I was working, and they certainly didn't represent the wonderful core conditions that I aspired to hold and show as a therapist.

It's hard to expose the things that you don't like about yourself or your work. Fortunately, my supervisor was warm and supportive. She helped me understand the importance of being aware of my feelings as I was working.

By exploring my feelings, and the behaviours they elicited, I eventually learned how each had some connection to experiences I had had in my life. The 'working too hard' feeling was connected to a deeply held experience of having to work hard in order to be loved. The tightness in my chest, I came to understand, was connected to an ingrained fear of being criticized for 'not knowing'. I also came to understand how, especially early in my career, these experiences made it difficult to feel confident in my work. My fear of being criticised, for example, made it difficult to have professional boundaries on things like changing session times, cancellations and sticking to time limits. Over time, I learned that when I am in tune with my emotional world, it can turn my head in the direction of importance. When I try to ignore it or shut it down, I feel unsettled and unsure. As I grew in this understanding, I became stronger and more grounded as a therapist. This experience was so powerful, that it led me to want to find out more about how other therapists experience their emotional worlds as they are working.

## Literature in the field

I'm in the early stages of exploring the literature to learn more about how the emotional world of therapists has been researched and written about. What I have learned so far is that the emotional world of the therapist appears to be either theorised in terms of constructs and theories often researched quantitatively (e.g., countertransference reactions, attachment style of the therapist) or somehow idealized – as in the conceptual writing and research on the core conditions that therapists need to imbue to build a strong therapeutic relationship or the theories of intersubjectivity or 'moments of meeting' that are presented as the jewels of our work. These constructs, theories, aspirations and ideals are all valuable in their own way, however my frustration was that they do not seem to speak to the everydayness of the experience of psychotherapists as they are working. My interest is in the normal, everyday emotional world of the therapist that is alive in the therapy room and is influencing their work with clients.

To better conceptualise what has been researched and written about, and where my interest was placed, I drew a bell curve (Figure 4.1). From the diagram, you can see how I have tried to define my area of interest as it sits with other psychotherapy research and conceptual writing. My area of interest is the middle of the bell curve – the emotional world we experience in the everydayness of our work as therapists – us as people, carrying our histories and experiences of relating, as we seek to do meaningful work with our clients.

The choice of a methodology for my research became clear as I thought about how I reflected on my own experiences as a therapist. I had to first have awareness that I was feeling something. Then, my supervisor helped me focus inwardly on the feeling that I noticed, encouraging me to put myself back into the experience and allow myself to really be in it. The feelings, thoughts and bodily sensations that I noticed as I relived my experience helped me more deeply understand what was happening for me. For me, hermeneutic phenomenology, a methodology that focuses on the pre-reflective lived experience of the research participant, most closely matched my own process. But pre-reflective experience is harder to get to than most people imagine! So, to help me better understand how to explore pre-reflective experience, my research supervisor encouraged me to start writing phenomenologically about my own experiences as a therapist in the middle of the bell curve.

## Learning to write phenomenologically

I am in the early stages of learning how to write phenomenologically. But here is how I am practicing. I start by reflecting on a time in my work that I noticed a bodily sensation, an emotional response, or a behaviour that I was curious

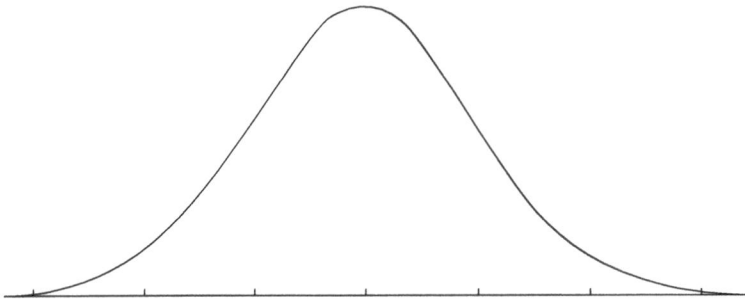

*Therapists' use of own emotions*

| Rigid adherence to theory, constructs, techniques and interventions | Therapeutic use of theory, constructs techniques and interventions | The therapist in the interpersonal space | Magic Moments | Transpersonal theories |
|---|---|---|---|---|
| This involves the therapist using theory or constructs to pathologise, explain or make sense of their feelings, thinking and behaviour when working with clients. | This involves the therapist using theory, constructs or interventions with attunement to the client and awareness of their self. | This involves the therapist being aware of and curious about their feelings, thoughts and behaviours in the 'everydayness' of practice. This is done without conceptualizing reactivity or responses through the use of theory or constructs. | This involves the powerful moments of intersubjectivity that could be described as the 'jewels of our work'. | This involves the therapist using theory and constructs that could be described as involving a higher self, the soul, the mystical or the transpersonal self. The therapist sees little or no boundary between themselves and the other. |

*Figure 4.1* Bell Curve of The Therapist's Experience, by Lisa Champion

about (such as talking too much). Sitting quietly at my desk, I close my eyes and put myself back into my counselling room. I picture the room, the client, myself sitting in my chair. I put myself back into the scene and allow myself to feel whatever it was that I noticed. I keep my eyes closed and invite the feeling to be with me. I notice what is happening in my body, I notice my thoughts, my intentions, my behaviours. I keep turning back to my body and asking myself 'what is happening to me right now?' as I experience this moment. When I feel like I have a really good sense of my experience, I open my eyes and I begin to write. I don't edit or re-read – I just try to write as freely as I can about what I noticed was happening to me in the experience. Sometimes I have to close my eyes and go back to the experience again to be sure that I am writing as close to the pre-reflective experience as possible. Later I go back and refine what I've written. Here is an example of one of my vignettes:

I am sitting here, in my chair, looking at you across the room. You feel large – filling the space with your voice, your presence. You are full of thoughts and story. I am, at first, trying to stay relaxed. I will myself to just allow you to be you, but in myself I can feel an energy, like a vibration. It feels hollow in my chest. It's like a giant hole. A hollowness of not-knowing. There is movement towards this hollowness – I want to fill it. I don't like feeling unsure, not knowing what to do. I am uneasy. On the outside, I will myself to appear calm. I say to myself to 'just stay with you'. But deep inside I am all over the shop. I am annoyed, with you perhaps, with me mostly, because I should know what to do. I should know how to calm you but the not-knowing in me is making me restless on the inside. The hollow part in my chest has an outer ring that is vibrating saying 'do something'. I try to breathe into this space to settle it. It helps a little. I ask you to pause for a moment and check in with your body. When you close your eyes and are quiet, I feel myself breathe more deeply. It will be okay, I tell myself.

---

## Activity 4.3    Reflecting on your emotional world: An exercise

- Choose a time in your work with a client when you felt an emotional response or noticed a bodily sensation or a behaviour that you are curious about.
- Sit quietly and close your eyes.
- Take yourself back to that moment. See the space where you are working, notice what is around you, picture your client, picture yourself.
- Now turn inward and allow yourself to feel what is happening to you.
- Notice any bodily sensations that arise, notice what you are saying, what you are doing.
- Keep turning inwards towards your own experience in that moment.
- When you feel you have a good sense of your experience, open your eyes and have a go at writing it down.
- Remember, you are simply seeking to write exactly what you were experiencing in the moment. Later you can more deeply reflect on what you experienced and invite meaning-making.

Lisa Champion's example illustrates how research can help us in our reflection-on-practice. In the next chapter, Biljana van Rijn will illustrate her approach to reflection in and her practice whilst introducing some research approaches. The latter will be explored further in the following chapters which delves deeper into research.

# 5

# Reflecting on practice with research

## Core knowledge

This chapter approaches research as an extension of reflective practice, with its ongoing attention to underlying frameworks and alternative modes of understanding. The chapter explores some of the following areas:

- Variety within research aims and focus, for instance: efficacy, effectiveness and practice-based research
- Links between reflective practice and research reflexivity
- Different strands within reflexivity, including introspection, intersubjective and socio-cultural reflexivity
- The meaning of epistemology surrounding 'reality' and how we experience and relate to it.

Making use of research is, as McLeod puts it, 'a valuable way to stand back from practice and to engage in constructive and critical reflection' about practice (McLeod, 2007: 23). The chapter approaches research as an extension of reflective practice, with its ongoing attention to underlying frameworks and alternatives modes of understanding.

## Different kinds of research

Barkham et al. distinguishes between efficacy, effectiveness and practice-based research. They suggest that all 'domains of activity' are 'needed in order to provide a comprehensive approach to the accumulation of evidence' (Barkham et al., 2010: 24).

- **Efficacy research** is interested in specific, measurable aspects of treatment. It focuses on the effects of particular interventions with an interest in questions of 'safety, feasibility, side effects and appropriate dose level' (Barkham et al., 2010: 23).
- **Effectiveness research** often explores the efficacy research in a wider context and explores if the isolated treatment effects can have a 'measurable, beneficial effect when implemented across broad populations and in other service settings' (Barkham et al., 2010: 23).
- **Practice research** focuses on variations in care and tend to capture and include differences and idiosyncrasies of everyday life. Barkham et al. assert that 'rather than controlling variables as in an RCT, [practice-based studies] aim to capture data from routine practice ... to reflect everyday clinical practice' (Barkham et al., 2010: 39).

The evidence-based approaches have gained a particularly significant influence.

## Evidence-based research

Evidence-based research is often connected to a scientific model. Stiles writes:

> The logic of the scientific experiment is that if all conditions except one, the independent variable, are the same, then any differences in the outcome, the dependent variable, must be attributable to the independent variable. For example, if one patient is given therapy, and another identical patient is not, but is treated identically in all other respects, then any differences in their outcomes must have been caused by the therapy. (Stiles, 2007: 123)

The RCT model involves the comparison of a randomly chosen 'case group' that is exposed to a certain intervention with a 'control group' subjected to a benign or placebo intervention. Questions in this 'golden standard' of evidence-based research can typically be answered with a Yes or No. Does therapy help? Does orientation matter? These kinds of questions often involve a focus on 'efficacy', which means 'potential to bring about a desired effect' (Cooper, 2008: 17). Aveyard and Sharp illustrate the process of conducting an RCT for weight loss programme:

> Participants are allocated into the different treatment groups of the trial at random ... Once each treatment group in the trial has been randomly allocated, the groups are considered as equal, and the intervention treatment is given to group one. The second

group receives either the standard treatment or no treatment or placebo ... The groups are then observed and the difference between the groups in terms of weight loss is monitored ... (Aveyard & Sharp, 2009: 60)

Typical for so called deductive reasoning, there is a hypothesis guiding the experiment with falsification as means of validating the outcome. Aveyard and Sharp continue:

[A] null hypothesis is usually stated when an RCT is designed. The null hypothesis states that there is no difference between the two groups. The aim of the RCT is to determine whether the null hypothesis can be confirmed or rejected. If the results show that there is a difference between the control group and the intervention group, the null hypothesis can be rejected. (Aveyard & Sharp, 2009: 60)

Some of the steps for conducting an RCT for weight loss programme may be the following, suggest Aveyard and Sharp:

- A poster will be sited in a weight loss clinic, inviting people who are interested in entering a trial to compare weight loss treatments.
- Interested people will respond to the advertisement, and those who fit the inclusion criteria will become the sample population. They will randomly be allocated to two groups.
- Group one receives the new weight loss intervention strategy. Group two receives standard clinic treatment.
- The rate of weight loss is compared between the two groups. Any differences will be attributed to the different treatments that the groups received. (Aveyard & Sharp, 2009: 60)

We will return to and expand on the issue of 'outcome' research later on. In the case study below, the BACP representative Charlie Duncan offers an illustrative example of how outcome research can be incorporated into practice.

## Case study 5.1

### Naturalistic study, by Charlie Duncan, BACP

This is a very basic example and it might not be as easy as this in 'real life' but it's one way in which data can be used to evidence what it is that you're already seeing in your service and how that evidence might then be able to make a case for increased funding. The British Association for Counselling and Psychotherapy (BACP) is a registered charity and membership organisation for counsellors and psychotherapists. They support practitioners and services to collect routine outcome data and can provide guidance and support in data analysis and interpretation. If this is something that you, or your service, would be interested in, please email research@bacp.co.uk.

**Naturalistic study**

A naturalistic study is one where the researcher observes or records a behaviour or phenomena in its natural setting, whilst interfering as little as possible. In counselling and psychotherapy research this might be similar to a service evaluation where the intervention and measures being collected don't change, but the researcher analyses the data collected to say something about the clients using the service.

Let's take a look at this example:

Alicia is a counsellor working in a community counselling service for children and young people up to the age of 25. At every session, she asks her clients to complete either the YP-CORE or the CORE-10, depending on their age and she also collects the Strengths and Difficulties Questionnaire (SDQ) at the first and last session with those aged 16 and under. Alicia uses the measures as a talking point during each session but does not score them and passes them on to her service manager. This is also how other counsellors in the service work.

Over the last few years, she's noticed that the clients coming to see her are increasingly distressed and many are on the waiting list for, or have been rejected from, a Child and Adolescent Mental Health Service (CAMHS). When Alicia raises this with her manager, her manager says that she has also become aware of this and has been having conversations about this with the commissioners in their local area. However, the commissioners believe that the interventions being provided in the community setting are for 'less distressed' client's and ask them what evidence they have that what they're providing 'works'.

Alicia and her manager decide that with the YP-CORE, CORE-10 and SDQ data that they collect as a service, they may be able to provide some evidence to back up what they're saying. When they analyse the data, they notice that 80% of the client's coming into the service are moderately to severely distressed, similar to those accessing CAMHS. They also find that 60% of the client's coming to their service 'recover', which again, is similar to the recovery rate in CAMHS. They go back to the commissioners with this evidence who agree that they're providing a vital service which can operate alongside CAMHS. They agree to provide the service with some funding, allowing them to employ two additional full-time counsellors each week.

## Research interests and focuses

The opportunities to reflect over practice through research are almost endless. Effectiveness and efficacy will, as mentioned, be explored in more depth in Biljana van Rijn's chapter about 'outcome' research. In this chapter, we will continue on the theme of human 'messiness' as raised in our earlier chapter. Like in the case study about Lisa's research therapists' emotions, the researcher's own involvement becomes part of valuable findings. Please read the examples below into more forms of practice-based research and consider, or if possible, discuss in pairs what you wonder about and might research in your practice.

> **Example 1**. Bernadette is a CBT therapist who experienced stagnation in her practice. When exploring her 'helper' role from a personal development perspective, Bernadette recognised how some of her own life issues had been put on hold. After revisiting her own experiences from adoption, Bernadette became interested in developing therapeutic support for mothers who have adopted their children of birth. As part of developing a research supported practice, Bernadette researches into the lived, phenomenological experience of birth mothers who relinquished a child for adoption during the 1960s to the 1980s.

> **Example 2**. Stephen is an existential psychotherapist specialising in young children and adolescents. As a manager for twenty years at the school counselling service Place2be, he is keen to monitor and evaluate the service to explore what works and why. He notices a plethora of evaluative approaches and decides to do a pluralistic study – drawing from co-operative enquiry, grounded theory and case study research. He is interested in the experience of teachers, school leaders, children and parents.

> **Example 3**. Alan is an integrative psychotherapist who teaches and works in a GP service with a broad range of clients. He thinks about therapy as a development of a stronger sense of self but is intrigued about what the idea of 'self' really entails. He thinks about it as a combination of social and individual aspects and has come to a point of mid-career where he reflects over and evaluates his practice up to date, hoping to be nourished by some new learning. He embarks on a doctorate where he combines his regular CORE-based outcome research with other forms of client-based research under the umbrella of narrative and mixed-methods research.

---

## Activity 5.1

Take some time and consider your interest and research question, with some different research 'lenses' and methodologies in mind:

- What might you want to research? What is your practice-related concern and query?

---

## Research 'life cycle'

We will consider research at different 'research life cycle phases':

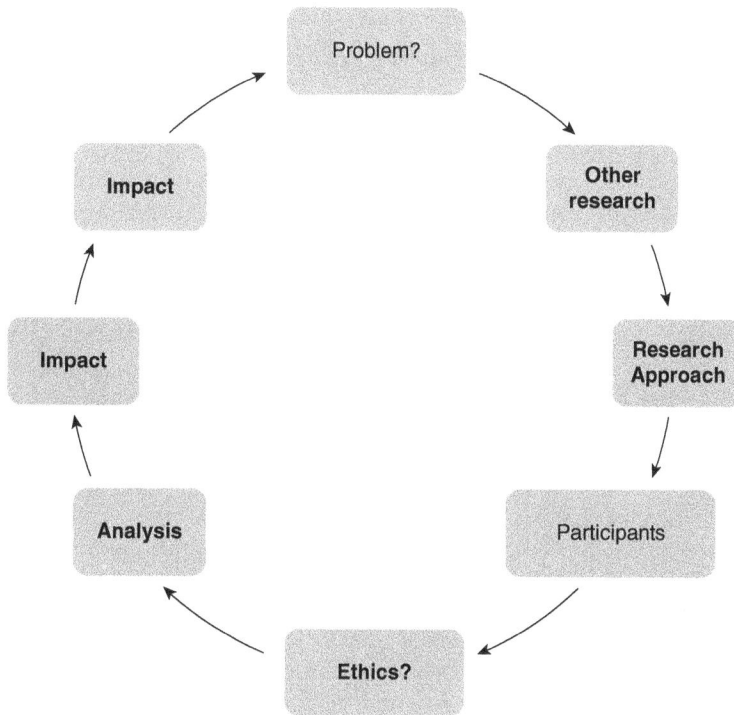

*Figure 5.1*  Research 'life-cycle'

This will involve considering some of the following stages:

- Problem in clinical practice
- Literature review
- Formulation of research problem
- Reflexivity
- Ethics
- Methodology and method
- Participants
- Research strategy: summary
- Information gathering, focus group, interview, survey, etc.
- Data analysis
- Impact

## Activity 5.2   Keeping up-to-date with research

We addressed the issue of literature review earlier. It is an excellent way of learning more about both our own and others' theories. A literature review

*(Continued)*

typically summarises and synthesises scholarly research in different areas and topics – for instance on humanistic or psychodynamic therapy theory or, as in this section, on reflective practice theory. There are however numerous ways of doing a literature review; in fact, Grant and Booth (2009) identify 14 review types when researching theory about literature review. Common for all reviews tend to be some form of search strategy which communicates what we aim to include or not include, for instance: only research written in English, published in academic journals after 2010, etc. It is important to have some form of audit trail for others to follow and validate the search. Making note of what we select and disregard will increase the validity and trustworthiness of your search. This can include notes about not finding relevant research via common search platforms, such as EBSCO, often covering predominantly quantitative research. Reasons for looking elsewhere will then need to be discussed in the text. Access to a university library certainly helps, but online search facilities like Research Gate and Google Scholar make it possible for anyone to access existing research on different topics.

You may remember how in Chapter 1 we shared our own attempt to update our knowledge about reflective practice theory. We inserted 'reflective practice' as the search term, choosing journal articles via the collective search engine EBSCO at our university library, leading to the standard search sites PsychINFO, PsycARTICLES/Psychology and Behavioral Sciences. We were interested to see how, if at all, reflective practice was referred to within and across different professions or disciplines. We also selected articles with an interest in later research, starting with an interest in research after our first edition in 2009, but gradually including earlier since some later studies referred to earlier which felt relevant; we continued our search in a 'snowball' way.

- Have you got access to any online libraries? Search sites like Research Gate and Google Scholar can also be helpful platforms for your search but therapist member organisations increasingly offer their members access to sites like EBSCO.
- Consider your ways of accessing information and make note about what you potentially need more support in. Discuss with your tutor or supervisor about ways forward.

## Research problem and 'lenses' to illuminate it

### Understanding and explaining?

Considering research lenses is essential, but it can also be easy to get lost in a dichotomy between approaches. Research is often distinguished in terms of 'quantitative' and 'qualitative' approaches. **Quantitative research** suits studies where generalisations and causal line of enquires are considered relevant. It is helpful for exploring *change*, correlations and questions referring to how *many* and how *much*. Questionnaires and statistical records are typical quantitative methods which help to approach large numbers of respondents with questions that help to transform respondents' reactions into numbers for statistical analysis. Its focus is in this sense on aspects of 'reality' which can be quantified, tested and measured in some form.

**Qualitative research** revolves, again as mentioned, around meanings and *experiences*. Meanings are approached as ambivalent and ever-changing and qualitative research adds 'three-dimensional' (Saldaña, 2009) understandings of people in context of their personal, socio-cultural, gender- and life-stage-related contexts. Qualitative research can be said to position itself in the gap between objects and their representations (Ritchie, Lewis, McNaughton, Nicholls, & Ormston 2014) exploring reality with an interest in how we experience it. 'Inductive' versus 'deductive' are other common ways of distinguishing between research, which aim to 'test' a theory or hypothesis versus research approaching its data with an 'open mind' as a starting point.

The terms **nomothetic** and **idiographic** are further concepts, suggested by Neo-Kantian philosophers, for contrasting approaches to knowledge. Nomothetic knowledge captures the – for natural sciences – typical interest in generalisations. It aims to explain categories and types of 'objective phenomena', for instance, with a focus on classes or cohorts of individuals. To have an idiographic approach means being interested in each case, with focus on each individual's unique experiences and meaning-making processes.

**Practice-based research** typically starts with a question related to our practice, either directly related to our clients – like in the example of Foziha Hamid's research which was borne out of noticing new client problems, in that case linked to the growing use of technology (see Case Study 3.6 in Chapter 3). The examples with Stephen Adams-Langley, Alan Priest and Bernadette Kane illustrate how research also often taps into personal queries and responds to a natural sense of both personal and professional growth.

**Each research question or problem requires a decision about research methodology.** This works as a 'lens' through which we agree to explore our problem. Our choice of 'lens' depends on the kind of problem we want to highlight and why.

Allport (1962), Ghaemi (2007) and Greenberg et al. (2003) are examples of practitioners in the field of therapy who support a **dialectic** approach to psychological processes, **a combination of knowing with and knowing about**.

Greenberg et al. (2003: 13) build on a neo-Kantian distinction between empathic understanding and casual explanation, and suggests that we sometimes can build, dialectically, on the different forms of knowledge lenses on a problem. Their example from a client presenting eating problems illustrates how a single loop, causal explanation can build as practitioners integrate other theories in the understandings of their clients:

> In contrast to emphatic 'understanding', 'causal explanation' is stated in scientific terms and is believed to follow general laws like those characterising the natural sciences. It deals with factors, generally biological ones, operating at an extra-conscious level that can be studied using experimental methods ... [However, when] we attempt to build up a picture of how someone's problems have evolved [we pay]

attention to their previous experiences, their vulnerabilities and resources and their current life circumstances. These features are particular to the individual and ... cannot be expressed in terms of general laws. The aim to 'understand' is, on the other hand, guided by interests into how someone's problems have evolved and are ever changing, viewed from 'their previous experiences, their vulnerabilities and resources and their current life circumstances. (Greenberg et al., 2003: 181)

Greenberg et al. (2003) also builds on Dilthey's idea of that understanding (Verstehen) and explaining (Erklarung) as two epistemologically different approaches to knowledge, which might dialectically nourish each other. Greenberg et al. suggest below the importance of a dialectic relationship between understanding and explaining:

The assessment ... heeds both understanding which is underpinned by 'reason' [and] empathic understanding and explanation, underpinned by causes. Both are necessary for a full account of the development of an individual's illness. (Greenberg et al., 2003: 13–14)

## Case study 5.2

Jane is 17 years old and suffers from anorexia. Initially, the psychiatrist approaches the new case with a predominantly explanatory commitment guided by technical reflections:

The clinical picture is typical of anorexia nervosa according to both ICD 10 and DSMIV (restricting subtype). She [Jane] shows a purposive reduction in food intake ... It is important to assess her serum electrolytes status since a hypocalcaemia alkalosis would suggest that she is secretly inducing vomiting ... Although she has not accepted that she is emaciated and that she needs help ... she admitted to a number of distressing feelings ... Her parents will probably also support putting pressure on her to accept admission. The psychiatrist will need to be firm ... admission under compulsory order might need to be considered. (Greenberg et al., 2003: 106, 110)

Jane actually did gain weight after two months as an inpatient. However, soon after her discharge, she quickly lost weight again. In accordance with reflective practice, the unexpected outcome calls for a new hypothesis:

In the first three months of follow-up treatment the hypothesis that Jane's symptoms served a function in maintaining the current family system was explored.

Greenberg et al. continue with references that illustrate double-loop learning:

The clinician reassesses the strategy and reformulates his hypothesis on the basis of a reflexive stance to Jane and the situation. This requires an ability by the male doctor to 'try on' the perspective and existence of Jane and her mother. The knowledge is transformed into practice with a new angle to the work with Jane:

It has become clear that both parents have had considerable difficulty in separating from their children ... There is some evidence that [the mother] may have failed to come to terms with the divorce ... Jane's mother now fears that Jane also will abandon her for her father ... her mother would then have lost both daughters. These concerns for her mother might have been sufficient to cause Jane's relapse, particularly if coupled with an equal wish to be with her father ... in fact, the illness has served as a tool to reconstitute the family ... The father frequently returns now ... The illness has also ended Jane's moves to establish independence from her mother. She has become clinging like a small child ... who needs to be looked after, even fed. Sessions with Jane's mother supported the view that there was a marked interdependence between them and that this was a contributing factor to Jane's illness. Their relationship seemed to require Jane to be a 'little girl'. (Greenberg et al., 2003: 112)

Greenberg et al.'s case study (2003: 108, 110) shows how we can expand on the single-loop learning about Jane with reflections that take her social family situation into account, as well as culturally transmitted values about women and their potential lack of power. The therapists looped back on the problem with a variety of influences in mind, including physiological, psychological, inter-personal and socio-cultural considerations.

Finlay and Gough's (2003) captures the human behind all our professional accounts. There reflections add the important personal involvement of the therapist in the reflective practice cycle. At the hub of the connection between the client and the therapist, there is always a human being:

[Jane] and I are masters at intellectualising bulimia. Through our conversations, I have moved beyond the literal interpretation of bulimia as being only about thinness to thinking about how eating disorders also speak to personal longings. But it always has been hard for us to focus on emotional issues. I have come to see this as a relational problem to which we both contribute ... Bulimia is about mess. [We] talk about, study it, analyse it and WE DO IT! As perfectionists ... we craft exteriors that contradict the mess in our lives. Still I know what goes on 'behind the closed doors' in [Jane's] life, because I know what goes on behind my own closed doors.

The dialectic nature of reflective practice often results, as explored earlier, in an integrative thinking on practice – a critical appraisal of our familiar framework tends to involve considering alternative approaches which can result in 'integration-in-practice'. Research can, in turn, ideally reflect this more holistic interest so that approaches are combined and add to our knowledge. Pluralistic and mixed-method research are examples of research which extend narrow thinking about one approach being 'better' than the other.

There are unhelpful disputes around approaches to knowledge, and Messer refers to a 'culture war':

For the past decade there has been a culture war raging over the value and even ethical imperative of … evidence-based practice … I use the term culture war because the controversy taps into broad worldviews in matters psychological that divide many [practitioners]. These outlooks include … subjectivism versus objectivism … hermeneutics versus universalism … ideographic versus nomothetic … and qualitative versus quantitative methods. (Messer, 2004: 580–581)

We can however trace this 'culture war' – around ways of reflecting over, understanding and explaining reality – back to what Kant once referred to as the 'battle about metaphysics' (1781: 61). It taps into questions running through history, surrounding the nature of our existence and questions about matter and mind.

# Epistemology

Dealing with 'real' life research will sooner or later require us to confront the issue of our own world view. Epistemology asks questions about the bedrock and the ultimate foundations of beliefs. The term epistemology derives from the ancient Greek word *episteme* meaning 'knowledge' and *logos* meaning 'rational'. Taylor writes:

Ontology is the meaning of human existence. Epistemology concerns itself with knowledge generation and validation, meaning that it tries to ascertain how to make new knowledge and how to judge whether it is trustworthy and 'true'. (Taylor, 2006: 88)

One significant and overarching distinction between basic beliefs about the nature of existence can be traced through the distinction between 'realism' and 'idealism'.

## Realism of relativism

Realism implies a world view where material objects can exist independently of our senses or perceptions. Idealism, on the other hand, argues that nothing exists independently of our consciousness and our mind.

The philosopher Rene Descartes (1596–1650) emphasised the importance of certainties outside of ourselves. He was a realist, who believed in a reality 'out there', independent of our minds and perceptions. He was also a 'rationalist' and he approached reality as something with which we could gain certain understanding of through reason inspired by mathematics and geometry. Many researchers have since engaged with his ideas, either to argue for or against the notion of there being a reality 'out there', independent of us and our perception of it. Descartes' 'method of doubt' (1941/2008: 23) was inspired by arithmetic and geometry, and reflects the attitude of the Enlightenment triggered by the scientific revolution of the sixteenth and seventeenth centuries. Descartes writes:

Arithmetic and geometry and other subjects of this kind, which deal only with the simplest and most general things ... contain something certain and indubitable. For whether I am awake or asleep, two and three added together is five, and a square has no more than four sides. It seems impossible that such transparent truths should incur any suspicion of being false. (Descartes, 1641/2008: 23)

Between these orthodox views on realism and idealism many variants have grown. From idealism, we can see relativism and interpretivism developing to emphasise our personal interpretive framings of experiences. Constructivism and social constructivism have also developed to highlight how social contexts and relationships form part of our interpretive frameworks. From realist positionings we can also see developments – for instance to critical realism – addressing a reality 'out there' which in turn will differ depending on who we are and where we experience it from.

## Research–practice 'gap'?

The discourse surrounding therapy has changed drastically during the last couple of decades: from being relatively steeped in mystery, to evidence and accountability having been put to the forefront. The impact of deep connection – both spoken and unspoken – still however underpins theory and practice across modalities in psychotherapy. For therapists focusing on meaning-making processes with an interest in affect, embodied and yet out of awareness-based responses will often be at the forefront. This can in turn come across as odd for researchers from other angles.

### Research validity

In quantitative and scientific research 'specificity' often refers to being *different* to what is 'normal' as shared or being expected. Sometimes specificity is used synonymous as being 'peculiar' in the sense of being strange or odd. The idiographic focus in qualitative research mentioned earlier instead makes the unique its special interest and focus; and validity in qualitative research includes its attention to 'specificity', 'reflexivity' and subjectivity (Banister, Burman, Parker, Taylor, & Tindall, 1994: 21). Phenomenology and narrative inquiry are examples of qualitative research which typically build on small groups of participants, with interest in the interplay of factors which may understand each person in context of her background, gender, time and socio-cultural setting. We will refer to narrative research in next chapter.

### The phenomenological, lived experience

Phenomenology is an important strand in both clinical practice and research. Phenomenology raises questions about how the lived world presents itself to the participant. Van Manen asserts that the challenge of phenomenology is to recover the lived meanings of this moment without objectifying these faded meanings and without turning the lived meanings into positivistic themes, sanitized concepts, objectified descriptions, or abstract theories. (Van Manen, 2017: 813)

This resonates with the mentioned 'truth' which we sometimes aim for therapy, which does 'not have the property of extension or tangibility' (Symington, 1986: 17).

In the example below, Paula approaches therapists' lived experiences. Interpretative phenomenological analysis (IPA) is a branch within phenomenology which adopts a 'double hermeneutic' (Smith, 2015) stance to understand peoples' lived experiences in context of their pre-understandings and interpretive frameworks when referring to those experiences.

In the case study below the therapist, Paula, has used IPA as an approach within phenomenology for her research into how therapists experience their 'blind spots'.

## Case study 5.3   Researching lived experiences

This study uses interpretative phenomenological analysis to explore integrative psychotherapists' lived experience of recognising a personal blind spot in their therapeutic work. The five female participants aged between 42 and 60 years have between two and 20 years' clinical experience. Each participant was interviewed on two separate occasions, with a period of one month between interviews. The inductive approach of IPA sought to capture the richness and complexity of participants' lived emotional experiences. Given the methodological challenges uncovering the implicit domain of participants' blind spots, researcher reflexivity served as a secondary but integral data source and provided the experiential context from which meaningful findings emerged.

Three superordinate themes and seven subthemes emerged from the interviews:

1. feeling under pressure
2. facing a blind spot
3. finding the missing piece and holding my own.

**Theme one** explores participants' loss of self-awareness when personal vulnerabilities are triggered by client work. It also describes maladaptive coping skills such as avoidance, employed to cope with feelings of vulnerability and shame. **Theme two** describes the process of facing a personal blind spot where participants recognise the impact of their personal needs and history on their therapeutic work. **Theme three** describes how self-compassion helps participants develop an expanded sense of self-awareness and capacity to be emotionally responsive to their clients despite their personal difficulties.

The findings suggest that when shame is hidden and unacknowledged, it impacts on participants' ability to be emotionally responsive to their clients' concerns. Furthermore, unacknowledged shame is a primary cause of therapeutic ruptures in their clinical work.

Integrative therapists' clinical experiences of personal blind spots. An Interpretative Phenomenological Analysis, by Paula MacMahon (2019).

## Therapists and research

Between 2016 and 2019 we conducted one narrative inquiry and one mixed methods study (where surveys and interviews where used together) into how therapists generate knowledge, with a focus on how therapists engage with research (Bager-Charleson, du Plock, & McBeath, 2018).

### 'Patchy', 'unstructured' and often 'informed by personal interests'

Our first study involved a literature review, which critiqued therapists' research involvement as 'patchy' or unstructured and often informed by 'personal interests'. Rather than drawing from research findings, the literature suggested that therapists based their practice on clinical experience, supervision, personal therapy, general literature and discussions with colleagues (Beutler, Williams, Wakefield, & Entwistle, 1995; Castonguay et al., 2010; Morrow-Bradley & Elliott, 1986; Norcross & Prochaska, 1983; Safran, Abreu, Ogilvie, & DeMaria, 2011). Therapists were also referred to as seldom reading research and not often instigating research (Beutler, Williams, Wakefield, & Entwistle, 1995; Boisvert & Faust, 2006; Morrow-Bradley & Elliott, 1986; Norcross & Prochaska, 1983).

## Therapists' own narratives about research

This first study (Bager-Charleson, du Plock, & McBeath, 2018) focused on therapists' embodied engagement with research during the stages referred to as data-analysis. This study was anchored within a narrative research framework, focusing on dissertations (n = 50), interviews (n = 7) and research journals (n = 20) across 19 cohorts on a professional doctorate programme for accredited therapists at Metanoia. Our second study was a larger mixed-methods study with a survey distributed across countries and modalities, with a survey (n = 92) and interviews (n = 9). The following themes were identified through the two studies.

### Theme 1: Discrepancy between therapeutic practice and research

The study suggested that therapists often 'felt overwhelmed' and 'confused' by how core knowledge in clinical practice seemed to differ from what 'research' typically would focus on. Most therapists aimed to keep a relational focus and to draw from their embodied and emotional responses as sources of knowledge, as in clinical practice. This was repeated in our second study, illustrated below in Figure 5.2.

**How did you learn to become a therapist?**

| | |
|---|---|
| Sensitive to the relationship | |
| Accepting not knowing | |
| Open for the unspoken | |
| Comfortable with ambivalence | |
| Good at identifying problems | |
| Adopting an objective approach | |
| Keeping a rational mind | |

0%  5%  10%  15%  20%  25%  30%  35%

*Figure 5.2*  Therapists' knowledge in practice

When researching, several preferred methodologies which resonated with their practice and chose, for instance, narrative research and phenomenology instead of surveys (Figure 5.3).

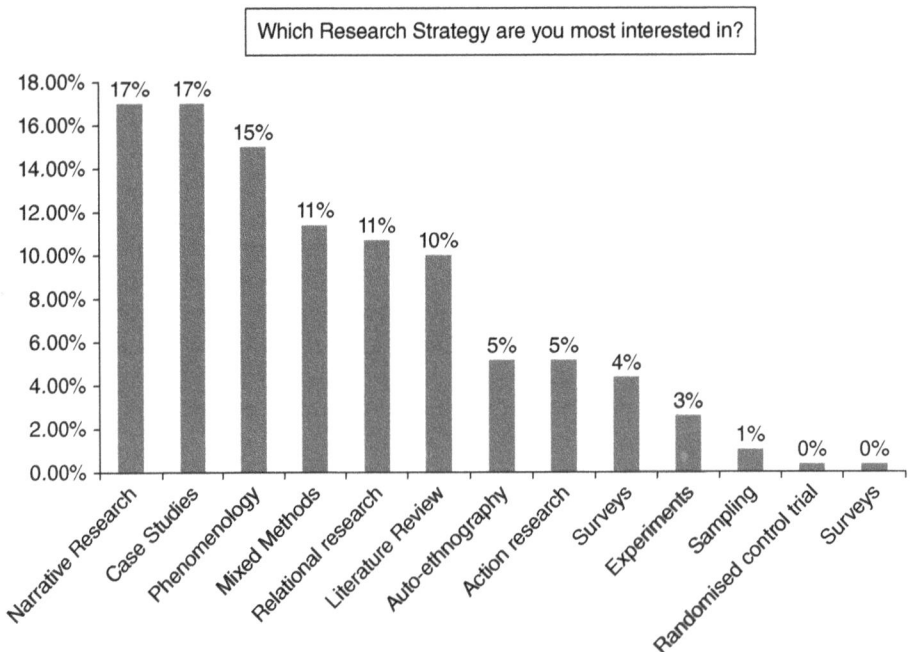

**Which Research Strategy are you most interested in?**

18.00% — 17%  17%
16.00% —
15%
14.00% —
12.00% —
11%  11%
10.00% —  10%
8.00% —
6.00% —
5%  5%
4.00% —  4%
3%
2.00% —
1%
0.00% —  0%  0%

Narrative Research · Case Studies · Phenomenology · Mixed Methods · Relational research · Literature Review · Auto-ethnography · Action research · Surveys · Experiments · Sampling · Randomised control trial · Surveys

*Figure 5.3*  Therapists' preferred research strategies

The focus on emotional and embodied self-awareness remained often in the research. Our interviews provided depth to experiences which the surveys only referred to in general terms. Some described it as 'losing' a sense of self when doing research. One therapist described, 'I became stuck at the structural level of data analysis. I had played in the words so much I lost sight of the body.' Another therapist said, 'My immersion in their stories [made it] difficult to "let go." I was overwhelmed by mixed emotions. I found myself laughing at some and crying at others.' Feeling lost and its impact on knowledge acquisition was tellingly captured by one therapist who reflected that '[it was] the task itself that was all consuming, rather than the meaning behind it'.

The stages involving 'data-analysis' showed a high level of stress, often coupled with shame and confusion; 'I underestimated the data-analysis,' said one therapist, 'you're desperately trying to find themes and codes and things but, actually, this is somebody's life'.

## Theme 2: Feeling lonely as a researcher

A fear and vulnerability around failure was articulated by a substantial number of therapists. One therapist stated:

> I certainly had not expected this experience when I embarked on the research and was taken completely by surprise [...] not only did I need supervision in dealing with writing a doctorate, working with challenging material, but also I needed personal therapy to separate out my issues from those of the victims.

The findings in our study also highlighted issues surrounding gender, culture and seemingly unhelpful 'stereotypes' in counselling and research. One therapist described her research as a 'secret hobby'. She referred to how she 'would only go so far in the world of research', choosing not to tell her counselling colleagues about her research interest:

> As a counsellor, and a woman who identifies as being black [t]here's a 'glass ceiling' ... I still feel there's a, you know, research is sort of about showing how clever you are, wanting to show off and all my whizzy little ideas.

## Theme 3: Personal and Professional change

Several therapists reflected on their experience of data analysis as something that facilitated both personal and professional change; usually this was after they had established effective coping/support strategies. There were several therapists who felt openly excited by research, one therapist said:

> Everyday I talk about research, I have become really passionate about the process, the exciting process about not knowing anything and then finding out, experiment with ideas and then finding new knowledge ... I find absolutely fascinating ...

Another therapist describes research as a significant part of her therapy practice:

> Research helps me as a psychotherapist to look wider. During one session, we come to find so much knowledge about one person. When I go deeper with research, I can understand the client better without getting lost.

Theresa, a play therapist describes research like this:

> I think about an everlasting 'research mindedness'. For me it's become an enthusiasm for 'finding out' which helps me to understand everything that happens much better. Every new client session leads to new readings, checking out of new facts and data. And every encounter with the data illuminates something new.

Some overarching themes were:

- Improving practice
- Developing new strategies
- Finding new knowledge
- Experimenting with ideas
- Understanding self and others in new ways.

Our mixed methods study reiterated a re-occurring problem from previous study in terms of the experience of a discrepancy between 'research' and clinical practice:

> 'Most of our therapy work happens beyond words,' said one therapist. Some referred to lack of exposure to and understanding of research, and one therapist spoke about her own 'closed position … because I don't understand the link'.

Not feeling valued as a researcher was a theme repeated from our earlier findings. Only 2 per cent answered that their research was valued 'to a large extent' by colleagues.

Similar to our previous study, active therapists sometimes address a need to keep their research interests to themselves, to avoid standing out! One therapist described how 'all [her] colleagues are scared of research'. Another therapist said that her manager has discouraged her from joining a training programme to learn more about research and, on the basis of it, making herself 'overqualified' for her role as a counsellor.

Both studies indicated that therapists often grappled with how to refer how they generated knowledge. The studies suggested an often experience 'research identity' for therapists.

## Activity 5.3

Return to the beginning of the section. Revisit the question below, with the examples from different research 'lenses' and methodologies in mind.

1.  What might you want to research? What is your practice-related concern and query?
2.  How might that question be illuminated? What kind of 'research lens', e.g., What Research Methodology, might 'throw light' on your question?
3.  Who might hold answers to your question? How might you approach the participants in light of your research 'lens' or methodology?
4.  What impact are you achieving with your research? What do you want to achieve with your research and how does this impact your choice of methodology?
5.  What do you need as support to start/do research?

## Relational and embodied knowledge

Clinical training and practice often, as suggested, emphasise affect, visceral and embodied responses as part of the valued intersubjective, interpersonal aspect of the therapeutic relationship. This is often a neglected aspect of research. The researcher Spry refers to traditional academics as headless horsemen:

> ... body in academe is rather like the headless horseman galloping wildly and uncontrollably to somewhere, driven by profane and unruly emotion, while the head – holder of the Mind – is enshrined under glass in the halls of academe. (Spry, 2001: 715)

Ellis and Tucker (2015) suggest that emotions are shunned in research in ways that contribute to the very prejudiced way that psychological therapies typically aim to avoid. They write:

> Just as individuals have been in need of taming the primitive and animalistic aspects of the self, one could argue that the discipline of psychology attempts to disentangle itself from the more emotional, subjective, messy and undesirable parts of itself ... The scientisation of psychology has to some extent repressed its emotional history. (Ellis & Tucker, 2015: 180)

Ellis and Tucker trace how emotions have been conceptualised over time. 'Psychopath' and 'pathology' are some of the concepts born from the Greek word pathos and the Latin word 'patior', which Ellis and Tucker follow through medieval theologies, enlightenment philosophy, biological understandings and towards affect theory and the development of digital emotion. Their review results in a conclusion suggesting that 'the scientisation of psychology has to some extent repressed its emotional history' (Ellis & Tucker, 2015: 180). Boden, Gibson, Owen and Benson give a good overview of literature in the field of feelings in research, and they assert that

> to understand human experience, we must understand emotional experience ... Without the emotional dimension of a personal story, understanding becomes difficult, spoken words become separated from what the listener understands. (Boden, Gibson, Owen & Benson, 2016: 1078)

Gendlin (1997) is another the researchers who focus on a 'felt sense' as a valuable source of knowledge. The importance of affect, embodied and felt sense in research have also been explored by Anderson and Braud (2011), Boden, Gibson, Owen and Benson (2016), Bondi and Fewell (2016), Clarke and Hoggett (2009), Denzin (2009), Etherington (2004), Finlay (2016), Finlay and Gough (2003), Gendlin (1997, 2009), Holloway and Jefferson (2000), Hollway (2009, 2011), Josselsson (1996, 2011, 2013, 2016), Orange (1996, 2009), Rennie and Fergus (2006), Spry (2001), Todres (2007), and Willig (2012). Finlay reflects, for instance, over her data analysis in terms of an 'attuned' process with different stages of 'empathic dwelling' [where] the 'bodily experiences' becomes 'a way of tuning into ... participants to achieve both a kinaesthetic and emotional sensing of the other' (Finlay, 2016: 23, 30).

Willig reflects over her embodied responses during the use of different methodologies, especially during her data analysis. The phenomenological analysis made her, for instance, 'feel like someone creeping along in the dark' (2012: 145), which 'grand' theories such as the psychoanalytically informed psychosocial model, made her feel 'speedy' by exhilaration and excitement around being precise and scientific and noting feeling 'carried away by her own psychosocial formulations' (p. 147). Metaphors and images evoke, in turn, emotions in the reader and helps to communicate these experiences and changes with their full force.

Within the framework of grounded analysis (Rennie & Fergus, 2006), this same emphasis on a felt sense is being made, as 'an approach to interpretation in which subjectivity is drawn on productively'. Rennie and Fergus (2006) also refer to 'embodiment ... accompanied by memories, images, associations and word phrases [as their] reservoir' (p. 496) for knowledge. Todres resonates with this, stressing that 'communicating understanding involves an aesthetic dimension in which what is revealed has the possibility of being personally appropriated ... within the realm of human participative experience' (Todres, 2007: 40).

## Reflexivity

Psychotherapy offers 'a very particular kind of relationship and a very particular kind of space in which we hope that new meanings can be made and new stories told, stories that may make life more liveable through an enrichment of meaning', as Bondi (2013: 4) asserts. To capture this reality in research, Hollway (2009) and Bondi and Fewell (2016) write about the importance of 'experience near' research about 'actual people' instead of aiming for a distancing, neutral research role. Etherington (2004: 19) defines this as a reflexive stance.

A common theme for all reflexive approaches is that subjectivity is regarded as an asset. The way we learn about how the researchers and their participants engage will help us learn more about intra- and interpersonal issues in our practice – and in life.

Etherington compares the epistemic positioning of a reflexive researcher to 'counselling skills [with the] ability to notice our responses to the world around us, other people and events, and to use that knowledge to inform our actions, communications and understanding' (2004: 19).

Reflexivity is an increasingly important concept in research. It originates from attempts to critically review the researcher's 'situatedness' (Haraway, 1988) and positioning within a study. There are now several definitions to reflexivity; Finlay and Gough (2003: 6) refer to different 'reflexive variants', such as:

- Introspective,
- Intersubjective,
- Collaborative, and
- socio-politically informed 'variants'.

They are interlinked and involve an interest into 'exploring the mutual meanings involved in the research relationship' (Finlay & Gough, 2003: 6).

## Reflexivity on introspection

This approach to reflexivity draws typically on the researcher's 'introspection' as means of gaining insights into 'a more generalised understanding' (Finlay & Gough, 2003: 6). Autoethnography and heuristic research are examples of reflexivity based on introspective reflection. They draw from the researcher's poems, artwork, diaries, autobiographical logs and other personal documents to recreate the lived experience in a 'full and complete' way (Finlay & Gough, 2003: 6). The researcher becomes the 'most important inquiry tool [and] "you" become a subject worthy of research' (Barber, 2006: 3). We will focus on research which relates to emotions in this chapter, and will continue with a focus on socio-cultural aspects in the following chapter.

## Intersubjective reflexivity

'Intersubjective reflexivity' adopts a sharpened focus on the interaction between participants and researchers, to use that as part of the findings. It brings in, for instance, countertransference into the research. The 'free association' (Hollway & Jefferson, 2000) interview and the 'infant-observation' (Bick, 1964; Datler et al., 2012) model are used as examples of reflexive approaches where transference and counter transference are becoming significant means to generate 'data' and new 'knowledge' in research.

## Intersubjective research in context

A common theme for all reflexive approaches is as suggested that subjectivity is an asset and adds to the findings. Both researchers' and research participants' idiosyncratic and unpredictable reactions and experiences are, in this sense, welcomed as valuable aspects of the findings just like in clinical practice.

In intersubjective reflexivity, the self-in-relation to others becomes 'both focus and object of focus' (Finlay & Gough, 2003: 6). The psychosocial research (Clarke & Hodgett, 2009) brings projection, transference and counter-transference to the forefront to, as Hollway and Jefferson address, an 'unconscious intersubjective dynamic' (2000: 93), where we often are 'influenced by our emotional responses'. Hollway and Jefferson suggest that 'impressions that we have about each other' often are 'mediated by internal fantasies which derive from our histories of significant relationships' (2000: 93).

They draw from psychoanalytic concepts to explore how both researcher and co-participant may be 'subject to projections and introjections of ideas and feelings coming from the other person. It also means that ... such histories are often accessible only through our feelings and not through our conscious awareness' (Holloway & Jefferson, 2000: 45).

Whilst originally understood as something which the client 'put' upon the therapist, 'countertransference' is, as explored in our earlier chapter, now often used in a broader sense, to also understand how the therapist's prior experiences impact the therapeutic relationships with the therapist's own history in mind.

Projections can act both as a resource (through, for instance, identification, recognition and containment) and an obstacle and trigger defences and mis-understandings in the interview. Hollway and Jefferson (2000) suggest, in other words, a similar view in research when focusing on how unconscious or as-yet out-of-awareness-related aspects of intersubjectivity might enter the research relationship. The section below illustrates this in terms of a mother–daughter dynamic. Hollway and Jefferson write:

> Jane and I were both white ... our class difference was stark ... I was probably close to the age of Jane's mother. I think it was this structural feature of our identity which precipitated the unconscious dynamics of which I got a glimpse in my unease about leaving Jane at the end of the second interview, [and when] Jane trailed off, I felt responsible for keeping the interview going. (Hollway & Jefferson, 2000: 48)

Hollway and Jefferson are, in this sense, recognising and bringing their own emotional response into the research, resonating with Price and Cooper who stress that both researchers and participants are exposed to 'unprocessed psychic material':

> Members influence each other intersubjectively and the observer too has no privileged uncontaminated position in the field. The researcher becomes a transference object for those inhabiting the field, as do they for her ... as she becomes entangled in transference – countertransference dynamics and enactments. (Price & Cooper, 2012: 64)

## Ethnography: Using infant-observation model in different settings

The infant observation model is, as Shuttleworth suggests, 'an ethnographic research method' applicable to many areas and fields of practice:

In recent years, infant observation has come to be seen not only as part of clinical training, but as an ethnographic research method that gives access to the psychological development of the infant within ordinary family life ... It has also been used as a research method in new areas of study ... as a wider social research project. (Shuttleworth, 2012: 171)

Infant-observation (Clarke & Hoggett, 2009; Hollway, 2011; Hollway & Jefferson, 2000; Urwin & Sternberg, 2012) is another example of research with an intersubjective emphasis. In their book about infant-observation as an applicable model in different areas of research, Urwin and Sternberg (2012) conclude firstly that 'the student tries to take an unobtrusive, noninterfering position, concentrating on the infant and taking in as much as possible of what is happening ... No notes are taken at the time' (p. 6). The infant observation method suggests that 'emotions, qua emotions, have to be felt in some way, even in a very mild identificatory way, to be faithfully recorded by an observer' (Price & Cooper, 2012: 57). Like in therapeutic practice, a significant aspect of the observation model is its use of others to explore the border between what role the conscious and the unconscious might have played for the researcher's means of generating new 'knowledge'. Like in regular infant observation, the input from 'seminar groups' play a significant role. Urwin and Sternberg describe how 'students are encouraged to make their actual observations as free from theoretical preconception as possible, and the description of what they have seen often have a spontaneity, even rawness, that may reflect the impact of the observation experience' (Urwin & Sternberg, 2012: 6).

The observation model has become increasingly used in other contexts where intersubjectivity and interpersonal aspects are underpinning the practice. The example below is from a nursing home, where the researcher follows nursing patients who are deteriorating for what staff have described as 'for no obvious reason'. The observer visits the home weekly and repeatedly records episodes from Mr Hartz's day-to-day life, as illustrated in the following extract by Datler et al.:

Mr Hartz is a tall, slender 75-year-old man who suffers from dementia and, for that reason, now lives in a nursing home. During the day he enjoys going for walks through the corridors of the dementia unit, but is otherwise barely able to eat or drink without assistance. His ability to communicate with others is steadily diminishing ... Mr Hartz is visited by his wife. The observed, Ms Ursula Bog, who visits on a weekly basis, repeatedly records episodes of tender contact between them ... The 12th observation, for example, illustrates such tenderness. (Datler et al., 2012: 160)

## Case study 5.4

### Observation notes 1:

Mr Hartz carefully reaches out towards his wife's hand. He lifts her left hand slightly upward and places it on the table. Mrs Hartz is still talking to the lady, while her husband turns her hand to and fro, again and again.

*(Continued)*

She then slowly reaches for his and holds it gently in hers. Both of them also put their other hands on the surface of the table and stroke each other's hand … etc.

### Observation notes 2:

Mr Hartz approaches me. He comes up very close in front of me, staring down my cleavage. As he does so, he smiles. He remains standing like this for some time without moving at all, looking at me. The short distance between us eventually makes me uncomfortable, and I take a step back. He comes a step forward, and again stands directly in front of me. Only after Nurse Martha has returned does he retreat from me, and goes to stand by the window (log, cited in Datler et al., 2012: 164).

### Comments

Group supervisions or research seminars play a significant role to throw light on and add new perspectives to the researcher's understanding. The seminars will aim to help the researcher to tease out meanings which remain on an enacted, yet out of awareness, level, particularly when there have been strong emotions involved and the researcher may have acted on a 'wish to protect themselves from more intense encounters with the painful emotions', as Price and Cooper (2012) put it. Their exposure to

primitive and unprocessed psychic 'material' becomes part of the findings, as typical for the infant observation method. The researcher will 'inevitably identify with research subjects and their ordinary defensive functioning in the field [and] will need the help of others who are not so emotionally involved with the material in order to rediscover reflective thinking capacity in relation to unprocessed … data. This is the function of individual, and especially group, psychoanalytic research supervision. (p. 64)

## Activity 5.4

Anxiety provoking and defensive reaction are expressions of subjectivity and can become part of the research 'knowledge' rather than being regarded as unwanted 'biases'.

If possible, divide into pairs:

- **Reserve ten minutes to think about an area in your clinical practice which you would like to explore further through research**. What are your thoughts about research? Have you experienced overlaps and differences between the way knowledge is approached in research compared to the way you build your 'knowing' in clinical practice?

Social background, gender, nationality and prior emotional experiences are likely to impact the research in terms of creating 'lenses' for our world view, but attending to how that happens will also add to the findings. Spry contributes with another extensive overview of research which incorporates embodied entanglement as a part of the process, especially in the field of autoethnography. Spry regards the 'the living body/subjective self of the researcher ... as a salient part of the research process' to study the world from the perspective of the interacting individuals (Spry, 2001: 711). Spry continues:

> I have often felt like I was speaking from outside of my body in my professional and personal lives. In fact, for me, academe has always been about speaking from a disembodied head. And because I often felt like I was calling out to my othered self, I never questioned the implications of a disembodying discourse ... (Spry, 2001: 715)

Despite an increased attention to reflexivity and to the researchers' positioning in the research, feelings still often seem homeless in research.

---

## Reflection

A common theme for all reflexive approaches is, as mentioned, that subjectivity is intended as an asset: the way we learn about how the researchers and their participants engage will help us learn more about intra- and interpersonal issues in our practice – and in life. Researchers' and research participants' idiosyncratic and unpredictable reactions and experiences are, in this sense, welcomed and valuable aspects of the findings.

- Consider your own positing in a study that feels relevant to you.

# 6

# Emancipatory knowing

---

**Core knowledge**

Some of the following key terms will be explored:

- Reflective practice requires openness for change. This chapter will consider change in context of 'emancipatory' knowing.
- The chapter focuses on the *TSS* in the TSS-ACCTT model, with an interest in challenging practice in context of its theory, role in society and the therapist's use of self.

---

Reflective practice rests on a critical appreciation of theory, self and the socio-cultural context for our practice. Taylor (2006) and Fook (2008: 14) address an important 'emancipatory' side to reflective practice. Fook (2008) stresses 'the capacity to question and change existing power relations' as part of reflective practice. Fook says:

[T]he critically reflective practitioner develops (reconstructs) their own practice in inclusive, artistic and intuitive ways which are responsive to the changing (uncertain, unpredictable and fragmented) contexts in which they work; and in ways which can challenge existing power relations and structures. (Fook, 2008: 51)

## Critically reviewing power balance

Power within the mental health sector is often 'inherent' but rarely explicit or easy to spot. We looked earlier (in Chapter 1) at Foucault's examples of abuse in early 'asylums'. The 'gay aversion treatments' offered by the NHS in the 1980s serve as more recent reminders of what from a distance looks like obvious abuse. Writing this book has also reminded me of the absence of women in science, philosophy and reflective practice theory, which until very recently included references to third person males. Penetrating Schön's theory highlights, in turn, how even those spending their lives addressing blind spots must see themselves as part of an ongoing – iterative and challenging, rather than 'once-and-for-all sorted' process. The chapter in which Schön specifically addressed psychotherapy is based on a male dyad of therapist–supervisor 'reflecting' over how a female client may engage in an abusive relationship in light on her own guilt for having sexual feelings. The session echoes some of the prejudices which Freud's hysteria 'treatment' expressed where the young woman's problem with unwanted approaches was explored in context of her own supression.

I have shared my background – personally, theoretically and socio-culturally – earlier (Bager-Charleson, 2010; Bager-Charleson & van Rijn, 2011; Bager-Charleson & Kasap, 2017), but keep realising that the way we position ourselves in practice and research is very much an ongoing and ever-developing process, influenced by life stages and changes – personally and politically – around us.

## Reflexivity as social critique

Whilst the introspective and intersubjective approaches to reflexivity mentioned earlier focus on underlying personal meanings, reflexivity as social critique will typically 'openly acknowledge tensions arising from different social positions ... in relation to class, gender and race' (Finlay & Gough, 2003: 12). Aguinaldo (2004) encourages us to critically review the power that different disciplines hold. Instead of asking 'is this valid research?' Aguinaldo suggests that we focus on what (and whom) is this research valid for? Aguinaldo challenges common concepts like 'health' through a 'social constructionist lens':

Health, like 'truth' – and thus, validity – can be used as a means to maintain unequal social relations ... '[H]ealthy' black men were [for instance] once conceived as those who remained subordinated by white supremacist rule. Political resistance to that rule (e.g., black slaves fleeing white supremacy) was viewed as a form of sickness – drapetomania. (Aguinaldo, 2004: 132)

Alvesson and Skoldberg (mentioned earlier) reflect on how 'male domination has produced a masculine social science built around ideals such as objectivity, neutrality, distance, control, rationality and abstraction' (Alvesson & Skoldberg, 2000: 3). This echoes with Spry's suggestion about a traditional, dominating Cartesian dualism which 'sever the body from academic scholarship' (Spry, 2001: 724), Spry adopts, as mentioned, a feminist outlook and emphasises 'enfleshment' in research, where the 'the living body/subjective self of the researcher [is regarded] as a salient part of the research process' when studying 'the world from the perspective of the interacting individuals' (Spry, 2001: 711).

This reflexive stance positioning knowledge in context of the knower and her/his gender, culture and class.

## Narrative research

Narrative inquiry focuses on how our narratives both convey and produce layers of understandings about self and others. Our narrative and stories about our own and others' experiences are approached as paths into how people arrange information (prioritizing, emphasising, ordering, etc.) and interpret (making good, bad, right, wrong, etc.) these experiences and events. Aquinaldo (2004) refers to an 'epistemological straitjacket' highlighting how restricted forms of understanding typically favour some and neglect or supress others. Our stories about self and others – who is good, right, bad and wrong – communicate both personal and socio-cultural values, beliefs and experiences guide our interpretations of events and experiences.

## Personal and cultural values about self and others

Narratives give form to shared beliefs and transmit values. It is an important term within postmodern thinking. Polkinghorne refers to the significance of narratives on both a personal and a cultural level:

> [N]arratives perform significant functions. At the individual level, people have a narrative of their own lives, which enables them to construe what they are and where they are headed. At the cultural level, narratives serve to give cohesion to shared beliefs and to transmit values. (Polkinghorne, 1988: 14)

Narrative research focuses in this sense on how separate and collective narratives or stories convey complex patterns about identity construction influencing social discourses. We mentioned Foziha's interest in developing support for women who had been abused sexually online; there was a lack of language to communicate about experiences from a 'virtual' reality.

The example below shows another study by the therapist Mirjam who develops therapeutic support for survivors of sex trafficking.

## Case study 6.1

### Psychological work with survivors of sex trafficking: A narrative inquiry of the impact on practitioners, Mirjam Klann Thullesen (2019)

This study contributes to the limited body of psychological literature in the field of human trafficking through presenting new and applicable understanding about the impact on psychological practitioners of working with women survivors of trafficking for sexual exploitation. Underpinned by feminist postmodern values, this study is shaped as a story of resistance against the marginalisation and oppression of women's voices. In taking a narrative inquiry approach to exploring both the singular and common experiences of impact, four women practitioners were interviewed, twice each. The design was collaborative, incorporating analysis and feedback between interviews, as well as drawing on poetic representation taken from interview segments. Each participant worked in different, often multifaceted roles, as psychologist, psychotherapist, counsellor and expert witness, yet all are psychologically trained. The three core aims of the study were, firstly, to expand understanding about the individual experiences of personal and professional impact. Secondly, to highlight the support required for practitioners working with survivors of trafficking for sexual exploitation. Through giving voice to practitioners, the third aim was to provide a new body of evidence in this much under-researched area, contributing towards improving clinical effectiveness. Across the four narratives, five different subject areas were identified: A personal philosophy, rite of passage, boundaries, protective factors, and knowers and not-knowers. These headings gave rise to a discussion of how practitioners are impacted in the immediate, on a psychological, social and embodied level, as well as longer-term. The underlying personal philosophies of practitioners emerged as both motivating and protective in the work. Pertinent was also how the impact of the work changed at different points in a person's career, the initial rite of passage representing a particularly challenging time in terms of impact and learning about boundaries. The individual understanding gained from the four narratives led to concrete output in the form of a template for a practice-based manual of recommendations, for application with organisations and individuals offering services to survivors of trafficking.

The case study below illustrates a valuable perspective on 'power' in the therapeutic relationship. The concept 'intersectionality' offers a significant framework to explore power from different angles, as described by the counselling psychology doctorate Sabina Kahn:

## Case study 6.2

### Research to reflect on practice, Sabina Kahn

This autoethnographic study explores how my personal narratives about oppression, due to my intersectional socio-cultural and political positioning within my personal milieu, relate to my experiences of power in the therapy room, both as a therapist and a client. What happens when I – an older, lesbian woman of Indian descent and an Islamic religious background, born and raised in South Africa under the system of Apartheid – am faced in the therapy room with another (client or therapist), who I view as differentially situated within the power structures that shape the societies we occupy? Does my subjective social and cultural positioning and level of awareness of my place/s in the social hierarchy, affect the way I conceptualize the psyche and its operation? Does it affect the way I experience my therapist, as a client, or the way I approach and understand my clients, as a therapist? Does it enhance that view or obstruct it? Beyond these issues, the research considers what might be re-enacted in the therapy process itself when the therapist is a member of or strongly identifies with a privileged and dominant group and the patient is/does not – and vice-versa.

Taking the position that identity is inter-subjective – that my own multiple identities, and consequently my access to power in its many forms, are fluid and emerging in relationship – the research sought, through a single participant autoethnographic design to discover how my own subjective socio-cultural positioning, ideological commitments and personal values might impact on the therapeutic relationship. My life narratives about intersectionality and experiences of power in the therapy relationship both as a therapist and as a client were therefore elicited through semi-structured face-to-face interviews in conversation with a trusted and willing critical research friend. As a therapist who has herself occupied various subordinate social and political positions and who has herself been taught to distrust and reject her own perceptions in order to capitulate to the perception of what Gramsci would describe as dominant cultural beings [...], I am deeply aware of the very real possibility that I too, as a counselling psychology and psychotherapy trainee – and in this sense, myself a dominant cultural being – could become so immersed in [...] the "authoritarianism" of my own worldview that I may not only universalize that view but also become oblivious that I am doing so. Thus, interactive conversations were also carried out with two co-participant therapists from my personal/social network, who share my beginnings in a particular historical, socio-cultural and political milieu in South Africa to explore similarities or differences in our experiences of power in our relationships to the other and the clients we work with.

We have looked at two forms of research which focus on understanding lived experiences, to develop therapeutic support. Both Phenomenology and Narrative Inquiry build typically on small groups of participants, with an interest in each unique case and the interplay of factors that may be specific to that person, in the context of her family background, gender, time and sociocultural setting.

## Phenomenology

Phenomenological research focuses often on experiences in our daily lives which are 'taken for granted'. We looked earlier how aiming for a phenomenological understanding often is an underpinning aim across modalities within psychotherapy, accompanied by the philosophy of 'reciprocal experiencing' (Rogers, 1961). Phenomenology is an umbrella term for research guided by interest into how things appear to us through experience; it requires an open stance to our existence and resonates, as suggested, with the therapy-typical aim of moving beyond taken-for-granted, unquestioned experiences in context of everyday human situations; aspects which may prevent us from 'experiencing experiences' as Rogers put it. Phenomenology raises questions like 'What is this kind of experience like? How does the lived world present itself to the client?'

Bernadette's research, as referred to in the previous chapter, revolved around the lived experience of birth mothers in Ireland who had their children adopted in the 1960s. Her research puts the variations within peoples' lived experiences to the forefront. In the case study below, the therapist John Barton (2019) uses interpretative phenomenological analysis (IPA) as an approach within phenomenology to explore the experience of living with an under-researched illness as means of improving his practice. His findings inform clinical recommendations for therapeutic support of an often misunderstood client group.

### Case study 6.3

#### Progressive (dis)ability: The experience of living with Charcot-Marie-Tooth disease, by John Barton

This thesis is an interpretative phenomenological analysis of the experiences of six women living with Charcot-Marie-Tooth disease (CMT), an inherited degenerative neurological condition with a range of debilitating symptoms. It is the first ever in-depth qualitative study into the lived experience of CMT, which is relatively common yet largely unknown. This is 'Paradigm II' disability research (Olkin, 1999) that listens to the voices of those with disabilities to advocate for improved conditions, services and status in the world. Those who are disabled are empowered to speak for themselves. The researcher, too, has CMT and another progressive neurological condition: Parkinson's. The women's stories are analysed alongside his own autobiographical narrative. Four themes are identified and discussed, drawing on literature from

*(Continued)*

across the fields of psychology, psychotherapy and disability studies: loss, discrimination, identity and growth. Arising from these findings, the concept of 'disability apartheid' is developed into a 'two worlds' model which can be used to describe how psychological factors such as acceptance and shame can impact the ways in which those with disability identify and engage with a disabling world and with their own lives. The researcher argues for 'one world' where all individual capabilities and limitations are respected. The findings also inform twelve clinical recommendations for counselling psychologists, psychotherapists or other healthcare professionals working with CMT, other neurological or progressive physical conditions, or disability.

---

We have so far referred to 'inductive' research with its focus on an open mind, and on how any patterns of behaviour or interactions should be made sense of from the individual's perspective. Reflexivity invites us to draw from our relational, subjective experiences as part of the findings.

Deductive approaches build, in comparison, on already formulated and 'tested' theory or data collecting tool to gather information to loop back on our practice from another angle.

## Reflecting on your theory

For reflective practice, reflecting on *theory* is fundamental. Theory-based understanding aims, on the other hand, for explanations. Stiles' theory-building case study falls within the category of what Dilthey referred to as 'explaining', asserts Stiles, who refers to 'explaining' research as aiming for 'a cognitive map of the world, a grasp of how things work ... following Dilthey [who] distinguished this sort of understanding as explaining' (Stiles, 2007: 164).

### Theory-building case studies

Theories convey principles and assumptions about the nature and sources of problems and guide our 'day-to-day and minute-to-minute clinical decisions' (Stiles, 2015). Good practice involves consequently making and checking observations so that we can adjust the theory in light of those observations – every time we amend or combine theories, we 'are privately engaging in theory building' (Stiles, 2015: 163).

Stiles refers to 'theory-building' case studies as a form of 'quality control' of our applications, modifications and elaborations of a theory. He refers to an 'ownership' that grows from deep enough knowledge about the theory, to 'recognize when the theory fails to account for an observation' (Stiles, 2015: 165). This requires background reading about the theory and good knowledge about previous research on the theory: we need to know the theory well enough to recognise and explain if and how our observations might confirm or contradict, or strengthen or weaken the theory, leading to increased or reduced confidence in aspects of the theory (Stiles, 2015: 165).

This level of knowledge about the theory also involves ownership expressed through the courage to suggest changes in the theory in response to observations (Stiles, 2015: 175).

## Case study 6.4

### Preparing for your theory-building case study

The example below is from a newly started study guided by an interest into how – if at all – a theory suggesting that past experiences impact present experiencing might be 'evidenced' in practice.

The study starts with the theory suggesting that 'current functioning is shaped by patterns and ways of being that were learned in the past' (Sills & Salters, 1991), with researchers from different theoretical backgrounds exploring to what extent – and how – this might happen in supervision.

### A case study into the impact of therapists' script and its emergence in supervision. An unpublished draft proposal by Charlotte Sills at Metanoia Institute, 2019.

Introduction to the project: It is commonly recognised that the past influences the present [...] current functioning is shaped by patterns and ways of being that were learned in the past, especially childhood. Each theoretical approach to psychotherapy has its own way of understanding, naming and thinking about this process, for example: script [...], transference and countertransference [...] – and so on [...]. Little research has been done to explore the prevalence and usefulness of these dynamics in supervision. The proposed research aims to explore this issue in order to develop understanding and theory about the processes by which the past influences the present in supervision – be that in parallel processes, proactive or reactive transference or other explanation. The research will explore whether and how it happens and, importantly, whether and how it might support effectiveness and how the supervisor might use it. The researchers from different theoretical backgrounds will take as a starting point the Comparative Script System (Sills & Salters, 1991; Lapworth & Sills, 2011) – a simple model which tracks the process of 'script development' from experiences in the past, to meaning making and pattern development, to here-and-now manifestation in internal and external experience. They will attempt to observe the application of this theory using this model to identify moments of 'transference' (in the supervisee or the supervisor), to observe how these moments are addressed or not, and assess whether they lead to insight, change and learning [...]. Methodology and research design: The proposed research will use a theory building case study methodology (Stiles, 2007). Two supervisors will audio record eight consecutive supervision sessions with two of their existing supervisees. Supervisors will write brief sessional notes after each session identifying

*(Continued)*

what they see as the key issue of the supervision. The research team would use the transcribed audio recordings and sessional notes for analysis. Supervisors will be invited to comment on the research analysis. Participants Supervisor: two qualified supervisors. Supervisees: each supervisor to follow the progress of one trainee and one qualified psychotherapist for a period of eight sessions. The supervisors will be asked to audio record the supervision sessions with two supervisees. At the end of the supervision session, the supervisor is asked to write brief sessional notes to assess what the key issue of the supervision was, choosing from a [specified, separate list]. We will seek to identify one or more instances of supervisee 'script' that has either a problematic or otherwise important impact on the therapy and/or supervisory relationship. We will then select and excerpt passages in the recordings/transcripts that bear on this script (and, if available, its resolution) for further study. [During the] conceptual analysis phase, we will link observations of the supervision process to the theory. We will assess where the theory has accounted for the observations and where changes in the theory (corrections, elaborations, extensions) are required or suggested. [Each] investigator will conduct each of these phases independently, maintaining his or her own separate written accounts (e.g., notes on observations, draft interpretations). However, we will meet regularly, in person or electronically, to discuss our observations and progress, and we will make our accounts available to each other, with the understanding that we are all encouraged to use the best parts of each other's accounts in constructing our own. Through this series of iterations, we expect the accounts to tend to converge. Eventually, we will combine the accounts into a report for publication. [...] The aim of this theory-building research is to develop understanding of the process of supervision in the psychotherapy field through exploration and development of the Comparative Script System theory as a supervision tool. The research questions will explore the use of the theory in clinical supervision (Is it used? How is it used?), and its role in developing the therapist's treatment range. The research will also explore the repetition of these unconscious patterns over time, and their assimilation process (Stiles, 2007).

Case studies give in-depth insights into the therapeutic process. The theory-building case study is one example of case study research that encourages us as therapists to systematically review links between observations and theory. You are invited to an informal theory-building case study, either on your own or together with peers, for instance in your group-supervision or possibly your personal development group.

## Activity 6.1  Your own theory-building case study

Discuss, if possible, in pairs, a theory which informs your practice. This might require some background reading about the theory and some insights into some research on the theory. You might return to the case study above for inspiration.

Charlotte Sills has chosen to focus on the 'Comparative Script System', which she has documented earlier (Sills & Salters, 1991; Lapworth & Sills, 2011) to track the process of 'script development' from experiences in the past, to meaning making and here and now manifestation in internal and external experience.

What theory might you chose, as relevant for your practice?

Apart from a solid knowledge about the theory, a 'prerequisite' for a theory-building case study is a rich collection of information about both client and practitioner. This includes, for instance, demographic information, presented problems and formulations as recorded through journals, verbatim transcriptions of audio recordings, process and sessions notes including assessments of sessions and the therapeutic relationship.

Chapter 8 in this book revolves around 'outcome measures'. How familiar are you with this? Stiles (2007) suggests using as many available outcome assessments as possible for theory-building case study research – with focus on both *how* the client changed (qualitative data) and *how much* the client changed (quantitative) – such as personal journals or diaries, poetry, artwork, letters or e-mail messages.

Choose a rich client case, which you have experienced as interesting or theoretically relevant: 'An unusual case can be as informative as a typical case [since] in contrast to statistical hypothesis testing studies, case studies do not require representative sampling' (Stiles 2007: 123). Look for 'basic facts' about the client and yourself: including demographic information, presented problems and your formulation. Draw from recordings of treatment sessions, verbatim transcriptions of audio or video recordings are a 'particularly strong source for grounding your inferences' (Stiles 2007: 123).

Stiles (2007: 127) refers to three phases of the analysis, namely

- 'gaining familiarity' through listening to recordings, reading transcripts and reviewing other material;
- selecting and deciding on a focus of the study; before
- interpreting, which Stiles refers to as the 'conceptual analysis stage' where you 'make links between observations and theoretical concepts' with conclusions about the match between the observations and the theory'.

This is intended as an informal exercise, where the client information remaining confidential or possibly used in agreement with tutors as part of your training. Please note that to disseminate case studies, ethics approval needs to be acquired. This is something which your tutors and supervisors will be able to discuss further.

We have spoken about inductive research as starting with as open a mind as possible, rather than being guided by a theory to 'test'. Inductive research is also often (although not always) guided by the above-mentioned idiographic approach knowledge, focusing on the unique, with an interest in the cocktail of complex components involved in peoples' meaning-making processes. Deductive research starts, in comparison, with some form of prediction like a hypothesis or a measurable statement. Often guided by a 'nomothetic' interest into generalisations across categories with some form of cause-and-effect in mind, this can often involve 'rigorous statistical testing' to explore and discuss 'possibility of these results occurring by chance [or not]' (Moule & Hek, 2011: 63). We look at this in terms of potential links between deep understandings and explainings.

Pluralistic and mixed methods can, as suggested, sometimes be a compromise.

## Theoretical reflexivity

Shared across all reflexive approaches is the interest in 'ambiguity of meanings [and] on how this impacts on modes of presentation' (Finlay & Gough, 2003: 12). This includes critically reviewing *theory*. We can do this as suggested in the theory building study. But we can also challenge theory on a meta-level, raising questions about power among disciplines and epistemological stand points. Qualitative research typically addresses such questions, highlighting for instance a neglected interest in the messiness of life and what we hold as 'reality'. We can also see strands within pluralistic and mixed methods research preparing for a more open dialogue across frameworks. The mixed methods supporter Hesse-Biber stresses the important emancipatory role for researchers. She highlights the power imbalance across disciplines and methodological positionings and suggests we 'lose boundaries' with options to genuinely and respectfully integrate different knowledge-building processes for an as broad and deep exploration as possible. She continues:

> Dialogue and reflexivity within and across research inquiry communities of sameness and difference can provide the ground for coming together to identify, challenge, and negotiate ... across methods and methodological differences and thereby providing the possibility of innovation and negotiation and a vibrant mixed methods community of practice. (Hesse-Biber, 2015: 785)

We can in this sense learn from different methodologies and disciplines, for instance from Sui and DeLyser who integrate within geography to move 'beyond the qualitative–quantitative divide' (2012: 112). They refer to how 'on the surface, the qualitative–quantitative divide appears as different methodological approaches' but also reflects a 'much deeper division in human intellectual endeavour and knowledge production' characterised by a '[divisive] chasm between scientific and humanistic knowledge' (Sui & DeLyser, 2012: 111). They continue 'divides can be just that: divisive. If our research and our discipline are to survive and remain relevant, we must move beyond divisiveness' (2012: 111).

In our study below, we have used critical realism as an 'umbrella foundation' (Creswell & Clark, 2011: 100) for what we described as 'multiphase mixed method' study with both fixed and emergent (Creswell & Clark, 2011: 54) aspects to its design. The study was born out of our interest in understanding more about the impact of training in multilingual theory for therapists practicing within that field. We hoped to combine different approaches for a fuller understanding of our problem.

---

## Case study 6.5

### A multilingual outlook: Can awareness-raising about multilingualism affect therapists' practice? A mixed method evaluation, by Bager-Charleson, Dewaele, Costa, and Kasap (2017)

Therapists are often unprepared to deal with their clients' use of other languages. This study focuses on therapists' experiences of having undertaken awareness-raising training about multilingualism. Did the training impact their practice? If so, in what areas? Adopting a mixed-method approach, quantitative data were initially collected via an online questionnaire with 88 therapy trainees and qualified therapists who underwent training in multilingualism, combined with interview data from seven volunteers. Having identified the issues on which the training had most and least impact in survey responses, the interviews were guided by our emergent interest in the impact of the training with potential relational complexities and unique, personal experiences in mind. A narrative-thematic analysis uncovered interrelated themes, relation to changes or impact of the training with regard to identity and therapeutic theory therapists referred to considerable transformative learning on both a personal and professional level, for instance in terms of how multilingual clients might bring different and sometimes conflicting ways of organizing events and experiences into meaningful wholes through their narratives during the session. Language switching seemed less significant in the survey, but emerged as a central theme in the interviews, especially with regard to the possibility of addressing, challenging and sometimes combining different emotional memories and cultural and existential concerns. Working across these areas triggered some therapists to consider the need for expanding their theory.

   [...]

   To gain what Bryman (2001) refers to as 'completeness' and a more 'comprehensive account' of training in multilingual therapy, the study has combined a quantitative, survey-based component guided by a post-positivist focus, with a qualitative, constructionist inquiry into individual experiences and meaning-making processes.

   Fixed methods designs involve 'studies where the use of quantitative and qualitative methods is predetermined and planned at the start of the research process, and the procedures are implemented as planned' (Creswell & Clark 2011: 54). Emergent design reflects the decision to involve 'a process that is ongoing, changeable and iterative in nature' as part of a 'purposeful and carefully considered' aspect, 'prior to, during, and after, implementation', as Wright (2009: 63) puts it. One such emergent component of the study has, as mentioned, been the way questions arising in the quantitative study has been

*(Continued)*

carried over into the qualitative inquiry. Another significant indicator of the ongoing, changeable and iterative (Wright, 2009) nature of the study was how the qualitative phase has developed with the subjectivity of the researchers in mind. The qualitative research phase was guided by a constructionist framework with 'relational interviewing' (Josselson, 2013) and narrative-thematic analysis (Braun & Clark, 2006; Chase, 2005; Bamberg, 1997). We viewed critical realism from a transcultural lens. Whilst inter- and cross-cultural theories typically highlight the significance of improved understandings and dialogues between cultures, transculturalism suggests that 'cultures are as much internally differentiated as they are different from other cultures' (Freudenberger, 2004: 39). We were interested in shared experiences among therapists with regard to their multilingual training, but we were also hoping to contribute with research about unique, personal experiences in the field. The qualitative section reflected our interest into this.

The following two chapters, by Biljana van Rijn, will expand on how we can engage around a research supported, reflective practice introspectively and collaboratively.

# 7

# Developments within reflective practice

## By Biljana van Rijn

---

**Core knowledge**

- This chapter and the one that follows expand on how different *types* of reflection can nourish our practice and how we can incorporate different modes of reflection into our daily practice.

---

The emphasis on reflective practice since Schön has influenced psychotherapy and counselling, among other professions. Practitioners adopting this stance look at the therapeutic engagement as a narrative and assume that they are part of the process that unfolds between themselves and their clients. Both the therapist and the client bring their own subjective experience and cultural contexts into the room.

My own interest in this field stems from my personal experience, which I have integrated into my clinical practice.

## Biljana's story

I moved to the UK from Yugoslavia in the 1980s. As in many such moves, this necessitated reflection on my personal and cultural identity. The civil war in the 1990s saw the disintegration of Yugoslavia as a political entity and I was faced with having to reflect on what this meant for me. I realised that every experience was subject to change, including certainties that most of us take for granted.

Reflection has helped me become aware of my own narratives about culture, identity and my own history. As the new political regimes started to obliterate recent history (even the names of cities from my childhood changed), I realised that my own experiences and memories, reflected by my family and friends, have survived the changes.

These jointly created narratives offered a sense of security and rootedness. I was raised in the cultural and political context of Yugoslavia, with its particular mix of people, experiences and languages, and still think of it as my country of origin, although it is not a recognisable political label any longer. My life in Britain gradually became another part of my cultural identity, and this integration informs the 'cultural lens' through which I view the world.

As a psychotherapist, I use this awareness of ongoing change processes to facilitate my clients' exploration of their own narratives to help them make choices in their own lives. Most of all, I hold certainties and 'givens' lightly, realising that everything is coloured by personal experience and culture.

From this perspective, I see the therapeutic encounter as an opportunity to engage in a unique process of exploration in which both participants take part.

Within this highly subjective enterprise, questions arise about how we generate professional knowledge to both enhance our practice and develop the profession as a whole.

Action research could provide an answer to this question. It is a broad methodology, which uses principles of reflective practice and provides a framework that can encompass different theoretical approaches and overcome the barriers between research and clinical practice.

In this chapter, we will start by looking at different types of knowledge within reflective practice and then focus on action science and co-operative inquiry as methodologies that can be used to develop clinical practice.

## Knowledge within reflective practice

Hoshmand and Polkinghorne (1992) suggest that the focus in psychotherapy and counselling training needs to be the development of reflective judgement. Practitioners need to be able to use different sources of knowledge to develop their practice, and this includes scientific or research knowledge as well as knowledge emerging from clinical practice.

# Activity 7.1

You need to do this exercise in pairs.

Take turns to tell the other person a story about your first day at school:

- first, from a factual perspective;
- then from your perspective as a child;
- and, finally, from the perspective of your parent or carer.

What are the differences in your stories, and what are the similarities? Construct a narrative using the view from all perspectives.

## Example:

*The factual story.* I went to school when I was five. I was taken by my mother. I left my mother at the gate; she was crying. The teacher took me in and I joined a class. I met many children that day.

*The child's story.* I was very excited about going to school. All my friends had already gone and I couldn't wait to join them. I was a bit lonely at home. My mum gave me a new dress; we bought it specially – it was yellow and had a little cardigan. I really liked it. It was warm and the sun was shining. The teacher took me in and I met all the other children. I saw my mother crying at the gate. I think she is sad about my father. She cries a lot. I felt worried, but then I went in with the teacher.

*The mother's story.* Since my husband died last year, I have spent a lot of time looking after my little girl. She is a great comfort for me. Today is her first day at school. I am proud and sad. Sad that her father won't see her, and it really hurts to let her go.

*The listener's story.* I hear that your father died when you were young and you were living with your mother. She was grieving at the time you went to school. You were excited about going to school and being with other children. It sounded like it was quite lonely and sad at home.

Notice differences and similarities in these accounts. What have you gained from hearing all of them? How can you apply this to clinical practice?

With parallels to Beverley Taylor (2006) mentioned in Chapter 4, Park (2001) refers to different types of knowledge:

- *Representational knowledge, a functional type.* This type of knowledge is usually generated in more traditional research settings. Counselling and psychotherapy have benefited from advances in neuroscience and developmental psychology. For example, neuroscience has helped us to understand processes involved in dealing with trauma (Cozolino, 2002; Rothchild, 2000). Developmental psychology and experiments on attachment have helped us to understand the impact of early relationships on the human psyche (Bowlby, 1969).

- *Representational knowledge, an interpretive subtype*. This form of knowledge focuses on developing the understanding of meaning. The researcher (the 'knower') is assumed to come to this process as a whole human being, with history and personal traits, which impact on the process of knowing. For example, the practitioner may use their own experience of understanding what it is like to be a client to help them empathise with the anxiety their client experiences in the first session.
- *Relational knowledge, a relational subtype*. This type of knowledge focuses on the role of human relationships. It derives from each partner in the relationship and 'stays with both to become part of them' (Park, 2001: 85). This type of knowledge resides in the act of relating and shows itself in words, expressions and actions within the relationship.
- *Reflective knowledge*. This derives from the critical theory tradition – meaningful human knowledge must not only understand the world but also change it. This requires conscious reflection in change producing activity. Action is an integral part of reflective knowledge.

## Case study 7.1

### Mary

Mary is a woman in her 30s. She is a single mother who lives with her eight-year-old daughter. She works full time. Mary values her strength and independence. She has dealt with a number of difficult events in life by 'getting on with things'. She has a good social network.

While she was driving to work one day, her car was involved in an accident. It was a sunny day, and she was enjoying the drive and thinking about her daughter. Another driver suddenly pulled out from the slip road on to the motorway and the subsequent collision involved several cars. Mary remembered thinking that she was going to die. Her car tumbled and she heard a crashing noise and screeching. Then everything stopped. When she came to, she was in an ambulance. Later on, she found out that her car was completely smashed up and unusable. She had cuts and bruises but returned to work a fortnight later. Everyone was very pleased that she was alive, but then stopped mentioning it. Within a couple of weeks, she became unable to go to work. She experienced panic attacks when she tried to drive, felt scared of going out or opening the door to strangers, and she was unable to go to the supermarket. She had nightmares about the accident and felt irritable and tearful.

## Activity 7.2

What types of knowledge would you bring to understanding the client in the case study?

- *Scientific knowledge.* To understand her issues, it may be helpful to look up research on the impact of trauma. Is it possible that her panic attacks and nightmares are in fact flashbacks? Could she be suffering from post-traumatic stress? Explore what your theoretical orientation says about trauma.
- *Representational knowledge, interpretive type.* Do you drive? Have you ever had an accident? What would you bring to working with Mary? Imagine yourself in Mary's shoes.
- *Relational knowledge.* How are you impacted by hearing her story? Pay attention to your sensations, feelings, images and thoughts.
- *Reflective knowledge.* Combine all these different sources of understanding. How would you approach working with Mary? Create a strategy.

## Action science

Action science (Argyris, Putnam, & Smith, 1985) was developed as an inquiry into social practice with the aim of producing knowledge in the service of practice. Practical problem solving within action science needs to be integrated with theory building and change. This is how action science aims to close the gap between research and practice. For a practitioner, this is related to the double-loop learning, explored in previous chapters.

For example, in order to address an issue that arises in the session, practitioners need to be aware of the narrative that they and the client are building and their own underlying theories of action. By evaluating these theories, they are further developing their understanding and their theories of action.

As a research enquiry, the key features of action science, according to Friedman (2001), are:

- creating communities of inquiry within communities of practice;
- building 'theories in practice';
- combining interpretation with rigorous testing;
- creating alternatives to the status quo.

These are described in the following sections.

## Creating communities of inquiry within communities of practice

Each practitioner using action science methodology becomes a researcher, building and testing theories of practice through their engagement with a client.

By doing this, practitioners conduct research in practice, as opposed to the research conducted by professional researchers in laboratory settings.

Action science aims to help practitioners to discover the tacit choices they have made about their perceptions of reality, goals and strategies.

---

### Case study 7.2

Sue is counselling Jane, who is talking about her relationship with her boss and his 'inappropriate attention' to her. Jane feels anxious about this. He often praises her work, smiles when he sees her and occasionally sits next to her when they have a break. She wants to know why he does this. Sue facilitates her, and they spend a session talking about his behaviour and motives. Reflecting on this session, Sue identifies that she felt anxious in the session. She identified the explicit aim of exploring the boss's behaviour and motives and an implicit aim, borne out of her own anxiety, to please Jane. She recognises that the impact of this was that they spent the session not focusing on the client, Jane, and her anxiety.

---

### Activity 7.3   Reflecting on a session

You can use this exercise to reflect on a session with your client in supervision or to practise in a peer group.

If you are in a peer group, organise a counselling session in a triad. Take turns to act as a counsellor, a client and an observer. Record your session.

If you are on your own, you can use this exercise to reflect on a recent session with a client.

Spend some time reflecting on your experience in the session:

- What did you think and feel?
- What was your sensory experience in the session?

Note down your reflections and use them to formulate what you think was the main theme in the session.

Identify your explicit and implicit aims and the rationale for them. What were your strategies as a counsellor?

## Building 'theories in practice'

Human beings construct theories of reality that they continuously test through action. The objective of action science is to make those choices explicit. Action science aims to help practitioners to infer theories of action from observed behaviours so they can be critically examined and changed.

### Case study 7.3

Sue felt uncomfortable after her last session with Jane. She took some time to consider why she and Jane ended up talking about Jane's boss rather than about Jane. Sue identified the avoidance, reflecting on how the focus had shifted from the client to her boss. The reflection led her to come to the co-created aspect of this process. Sue realised that her anxiety and fear of being seen as 'inappropriate' if she misjudged the relationship between her and the client, in some ways, mirrored the relationship the client had with her boss. She also recognised her own fear of being criticised, stemming to her own upbringing. She used the transactional analysis concept of 'psychological games' (Berne, 1964; Hargaden & Sills, 2002), which describes the interlocking of unconscious relationship blueprints in the current reality, in order to identify the dynamic and the possible outcome of this process. Bringing the unconscious into her awareness led her to wonder about Jane's fear of criticism.

### Reflection

Return to your group reflection in the earlier activity.

- Which theoretical concept would you use to describe the main theme of the session?
- What is your rationale for choosing that particular concept?
- Think of your interactions with the client and reflect on this part of your experience.
- Which theoretical concept would you use to understand this interaction and why?

Is there anything you'd like to change about it?

## Combining interpretation with rigorous testing

In order to validate our understanding it is important that our personal interpretations are transparent and tested intersubjectively.

### Case study 7.4

Sue shared this experience in her supervision group. Each of her peers responded differently to her presentation of the client. Mark fed back his

*(Continued)*

experience of irritation about the client's interpretation of events. Magda empathised with the client's sense of hopelessness. Each of them recognised how their personal history impacted on their interpretation of the session. Sue became aware that her client's interpretation of the behaviour of her boss, as well as her own acceptance of it, were rooted in their individual experiences. This led her to wonder what they might have missed in focusing on her boss's motives.

## Creating alternatives to the status quo

The aim of action science is not to facilitate knowledge per se, but to facilitate change for the benefit of the client and the wider community.

### Case study 7.5

Sue explored the session from different angles: her own and her peers' subjective experiences; interaction with the client; and theoretical concepts she used. She decided in the next session to feed back to the client that she realised that in thinking about her boss's behaviour and motives, they had missed exploring what went on for Jane. She would hold her own hypothesis about fear of criticism, in case this was not Jane's fear.

### Activity 7.4

Reserve some time to consider your own group work from Activity 7.2 and compare it with how Sue has processed her session with Jane. How does your strategy differ and how does it overlap with Sue's? How do you normally develop a strategy? Does your strategy usually involve the stages referred to here, or do you assess and resolve work differently?

## Co-operative inquiry

Co-operative inquiry is a development within action research that focuses on addressing the power differential between a researcher (practitioner) and a participant (client). It concerns itself with the ethical issues regarding the ownership of the process. Who defines what happened?

Heron and Reason (2001) define co-operative inquiry as a way of working with other people to develop an understanding of one's own life and develop creative ways of looking at things as well as learning how to create changes. We can use this approach in clinical practice to understand that the therapist and the client are impacted by the therapeutic process and changed by it.

These are some of the characteristics of co-operative inquiry:

- All active subjects are fully involved as co-researchers. All participants take part in reflection and conclusions drawn from the process. If we look at therapy in this way, both the therapist and the client are involved in developing meaning within the sessions.
- Co-operative inquiry involves an interplay between reflection, experience and action. In clinical practice, both the therapist and the client are involved in reflection about the process. The practitioner might use a reflective diary, reflection in supervision, personal therapy and overt review sessions with a client. For the client this could also involve a personal diary and review session. Questionnaires could also form a part of this reflection.
- The experience involves action and changes in the outside world. This may be particularly relevant for the client. However, the therapist could also apply the learning from each client to their practice and their own life.
- The cycles of reflection, experience and action are repeated several times. The knowledge developed within this process can take different forms – words, concepts, expressions – and diverse skills – intrapsychic, interpersonal, etc. In clinical practice, this means that both the therapist and the client will be reflecting on all of their experiential knowledge and using a full range of their human capacities.
- This type of inquiry can be informative (undertaken for the purpose of developing knowledge), or transformative. Transformative inquiry is particularly related to clinical practice and means that both the therapist and the client will to some extent be changed by their encounter.

Reflecting on this, we can ask ourselves whether knowledge developed in this way is valid.

## Validity in co-operative inquiry

The notion of validity is one of the key concepts in research and the development of wider professional knowledge. However, the concept of validity in such an experiential inquiry is different from that of the traditional positivist research. Validity in this context depends on the ability of the participants to be reflexive and transparent about their knowledge. We do not aim to find absolute truths but to engage in ongoing cycles of inquiry and change.

The concept of mentalisation as an ability to think explicitly about the states of mind developed by Fonagy (Fonagy, Gergeley, Jurist, & Target, 2002) refers to this type of thinking. In psychotherapy and counselling, we can use theoretical concepts to help with this type of reflection.

One of the methods that can be used to develop the depth of reflection and open up the richness of personal experience is interpersonal process recall, or IPR (Kagan, 1967). This method involves live recollection of any interpersonal process and enquires into the subjective experience of each participant. The reflection is facilitated by a set of questions that serve as prompts in recalling the experience and deepening the reflection. Some examples of the questions that can be used to help the client and the therapist to recall the session are given in the research summary box on interpersonal process recall.

## Interpersonal process recall – inquirer's prompts

The purpose of these questions is to give clients and therapists space to explore the feelings and thoughts they were experiencing at the time of the original interaction. There are two roles:

* recaller – the person who is remembering the session – could be a therapist or a client; the recaller is in charge of the overall process;
* inquirer – the person who is using the questions to facilitate the recollection – the role of the inquirer is not to interpret or judge anything the recaller is saying.

---

### Questions

1. Self-exploration
   * What thoughts and feelings did you have at the time?
   * Do you recall any physical sensations?

2. View of others
   * Did you have any feelings towards the other person?
   * What do you think they thought about you?

3. Own behaviour
   * Anything you were not saying?
   * Anything got in the way of how you wanted to be?

4. Values and assumptions
   * Anything you liked about what was happening?
   * Was anything taken for granted?

5. Social and physical environment
   * Did the setting affect you in any way?

6. Hopes and intentions
   * What did you hope to achieve, communicate?
   * How did you want the others to see/feel towards you?
   * Anything you would like to have said/done but felt unable to?

7. Past experience
  - Has this happened to you before?
  - Did the other's physical appearance/posture have any effect on you?

8. Reflection
  - Any idea how you came to do that?
  - Can you make any sense of that?

9. Closure
  - Anything else?

## Example

*Recaller (client):*   I remember sitting at the chair, thinking, 'I don't know what to talk about.' I was thinking about my week. Remembering bits and pieces.

*Inquirer:*   Do you remember any feelings or sensations?

*Recaller (client):*   Slightly nervous, a bit too warm, sweating a bit. Then I said I wanted to talk about what happened at work that week. I remember looking at Mark (the therapist); he seemed a bit tense, but he had a sort of kind look in his eyes. I liked him. He seemed relieved when I said I wanted to talk about work, and I thought to myself that's OK then.

*Inquirer:*   Was there anything you were not saying?

*Recaller (client):*   I wanted to make it OK for him. He seems very young and I sort of didn't want to upset him, bring anything too complicated. I don't know him that well. I didn't want to be too much …

## Activity 7.5

This exercise can be done in a triad with your peers. You can take turns to act as client, counsellor and observer.

- Client and counsellor engage in a practice session. The session is recorded. For the purpose of the IPR, once the session is finished both the counsellor and the client take the role of recaller. The observer becomes the inquirer.
- The inquirer plays the recording to the recaller (client). The recaller focuses on any memories of the session, aided by the recording, and recalls the session. The inquirer uses the questions to help the recaller remember the session.

*(Continued)*

> • Take turns so that both the counsellor and the client have an opportunity to explore their experience. The role of the inquirer is simply to facilitate and prompt, not to provide interpretations.
>
> Take 30 minutes each to recall the session and then discuss this experience as a group.
> As a group, discuss and agree what happened, and choose theoretical concepts to help you to conceptualise what happened in the session.
> Share what you learned from this experience with each other.

There are multiple sources of knowledge we can use to enhance clinical practice. We can draw on the epistemology of action research to help us reflect on these different areas of experience and knowledge. Park (2001) separates them into:

• representational knowledge: functional type usually generated in traditional research;
• representational knowledge: interpretive type focused on developing the understanding of meaning and involving the person of the practitioner;
• relational knowledge, which resides in the act of relating and shows itself in words, expressions and actions within the relationship;
• reflective knowledge, which emphasises the role of knowledge in creating change.

Different approaches within action research can be used to develop our practice and help us to develop it by engaging in cycles of reflection, action and evaluation. Action science (Argyris et al., 1985) and co-operative inquiry (Heron & Reason, 2001) are two methodologies within action research that can be used in this way.

# 8

# Evaluating our practice

## By Biljana van Rijn

---

**Core knowledge**

- In this chapter, I will present a brief overview of psychotherapy outcome research, its impact on national policies about the provision of counselling and psychotherapy, and relevance for clinical practice.
- We will focus on evaluation of practice using standardised questionnaires relationally and reflexively, in order to support therapists in collecting feedback and dealing with ruptures, developing collaboration and engagement within the therapeutic process, and meta-therapeutic dialogue.

---

Numerous therapeutic approaches and theories co-exist in psychotherapy, and their number is increasing. This understandably raises questions for statutory and health authorities in different countries with the aim to, on the one hand, provide best treatments, and to protect the public, on the other. Psychotherapy inconveniently bridges different fields. It is most closely linked to psychology, but also to philosophy and psychiatry (as a mental health treatment). This has led to some difficulties in evaluating its effectiveness in general. The methodology of randomised control trials, with high levels of internal validity, has mostly been conducted within health settings and has been most suited to short-term psychotherapies, where treatment could be readily man-ualised, and where funding was available. The field of humanistic, experiential and integrative psychotherapies, usually practised in non-statutory practice settings, such as voluntary agencies and private practice has not had either access to the research funding or methodological expertise held at universities and the health sector.

## Effectiveness of psychotherapy

Decades of outcome research into the effectiveness of psychotherapy have led to the recent publication by the reputable American Psychological Association, recognising its effectiveness as a treatment (American Psychological Association, 2013). The definition of psychotherapy they adopted stated that:

> Psychotherapy is the informed and intentional application of clinical methods and interpersonal stances derived from established psychological principles for the purpose of assisting people to modify their behaviours, cognitions, emotions, and/or other personal characteristics in directions that the participants deem desirable. (Norcross, 1990)

Meta-analytic studies (Smith & Glass, 1977; Smith, Glass, & Miller, 1980; Wampold, 2001) have been cited, amongst other research, as the rationale for this decision. Since then, further meta-analysis (Wampold & Imel, 2015) con-tinues to confirm the general effectiveness of psychotherapy. These studies (and many others), do not emphasise the effectiveness of one therapeutic approach over another. The majority of studies have found the equivalence of therapeutic outcomes amongst psychotherapies, leading to the much quoted Dodo Bird Verdict given by Saul Rosenzweig in 1936. Instead, they recognise the well-researched factors in effectiveness, namely, the therapeutic relation-ship (Cuijpers, van Straten, & Andersson, 2008; Lambert & Barley, 2002; Norcross & Lambert, 2018) and the aims of psychotherapy to provide relief from suffering within a health setting, with a qualified practitioner using a well-defined psychological theory based on psychological principles.

Research on effectiveness of humanistic and experiential psychotherapies (HEP) is also growing. A recent review (Elliott, Watson, Greenberg, Timulak, & Freire, 2013), which evidences HEPs successful outcomes in terms of the cli-ent's tendency for growth, shows large pre- and post-therapy gains through the empathic relationship (Connell, Barkham, & Mellor-Clark, 2008; Stiles, Barkham, Mellor-Clark, & Connell, 2008; Stiles, Barkham, Twigg, Mellor-Clark, & Cooper, 2006).

## Impact of research on practice

Psychotherapy research has not traditionally had much impact on psychother-apy training and practice. The complexity of statistical and research designs used in efficacy and meta-analytic studies requires specialised research skills and access to research funding, not usually accessible in ordinary practice settings. The design of randomised control trials focuses on internal validity, ensuring that research is objective and replicable. Unfortunately, this has limited its usefulness in practice although it has had a significant impact on the provision of psychotherapy and counselling within statutory settings and has been used to develop clinical guidelines (National Institute for Health and Care Excellence, forthcoming; National Institute for Health and Clinical Excellence, 2004, 2009). Clinical guidelines for psychotherapy and counselling, like those in medicine, are based on single disorders and recommend treatments with a specific research evidence base (such as CBT or IPT). However, this approach to psychotherapy research has led to notable omissions (Wampold & Imel, 2015) in terms of the experience of the client as a person (rather than just treatment of symptoms), therapists and therapeutic relationships, and research demonstrating equivalence of outcomes between approaches.

## Therapeutic relationships

Therapeutic relationship is one of the most recognised common factors in psychotherapy linked to outcomes (Lambert & Barley, 2002; Norcross, 2011; Norcross & Lambert, 2018; Wampold & Imel, 2015). However, it is less clear how to separate the therapeutic relationship from what therapists do in sessions (therapeutic method). Acknowledging that, Norcross and Lambert in their latest meta-analysis state that all treatment methods have a relational aspect (Norcross & Lambert, 2018). This is clearly the case in practice, where interventions emerge in the context of the session, in the co-created relationship between the therapist and the client. Some aspects of the therapeutic relationship have good levels of research evidence in relation to outcomes. They are:

- Therapeutic alliance (Horvath, Del Re, Fluckiger, & Symonds, 2011; Huang, Hill, & Gelso, 2013).
- Therapist responsiveness (Norcross, 2002; Norcross & Lambert, 2018).
- Empathy (Elliott, Bohart, Watson, & Murphy, 2018).
- Agreement on goals and a timely repair of ruptures (Safran, Muran, & Eubanks-Carter, 2011).

All of them imply agency, reflection and activity by both therapists and clients.

## Client factors

Despite the aims of statutory services like the NHS to provide individualised care, the prescriptiveness of clinical guidelines and evaluation of efficacy treats psychotherapy clients as passive recipients of 'treatment'. However, as well as research on the importance of therapeutic relationship on outcomes, there is now a body of research that confirms the accepted clinical wisdom that clients are active agents in the therapeutic process (Bohart & Greaves Wade, 2013). In their review of research on client factors in psychotherapy in the 6th edition of the *Handbook of Psychotherapy and Behaviour Change* (Lambert, 2013), Bohart and Greaves Wade conclude that clients' agency, motivation, attachment styles, preferences, as well as their levels of distress at entering psychotherapy, are all linked to outcomes, as well as early termination, which frequently occurs when clients are not willing to engage and invest in resolving alliance ruptures.

## Therapist factors

Research shows us that therapists' vary in effectiveness between each other and with different clients in naturalistic settings (Baldwin & Imel, 2013; Wampold & Imel, 2015). Wampold and Imel report the variance of between 3 and 7 per cent, higher than the variance in different theoretical orientations. Research on psychotherapy relationships and the therapist role in facilitating the therapeutic alliance, repairing ruptures and dealing with feedback further highlight the importance of therapist behaviour, reflexivity and openness. In summarising negative behaviours by therapists, Norcross and Lambert (2018) name therapist arrogance and therapist-centricity exemplified by assumptions, rigidity and impositions of the therapist's cultural beliefs.

## Feedback in psychotherapy

In view of the research above, it becomes clear that active engagement in therapeutic relationship and the importance of understanding the client's experience is paramount in good practice. It is likely that most training programmes, as well as qualified psychotherapists, would say that this is central to their work. However, actively seeking feedback from clients on their experience and preferences is not as evident.

Part of the significance of feedback relates to the recognition of the impact of our interventions and the need to adapt our work to help clients achieve their aims. Therapists have long been alert to this, and various methods of reflecting on the psychotherapy processes and outcomes have become embedded into psychotherapy training and practice. Students are observed in their practice sessions during training. Many of them audio-record their sessions, and all have supervision and personal psychotherapy. This suggests that we already have multiple methods and skills in assessing the effectiveness of our practice and our abilities.

Unfortunately, research suggests that this is not as effective as we might think. Psychotherapists seem to suffer from a self-assessment bias similar to that found in other professions. Research by Walfish, McAlister, O'Donnell, & Lambert (2012) found that most participants rated their own skills as above average in comparison to their peers. The therapists thought that only 3.66 per cent of their clients deteriorated during therapy, and 47.7 per cent of the sample said that none of their clients deteriorated. Similar results were found in other studies (Lambert & Shimokawa, 2011; Lambert et al., 2002).

These evaluations seem to be very inaccurate when compared to actual psychotherapy outcomes. Psychotherapy outcomes research shows that, on average, only about 40 per cent of clients achieve clinically significant change, and up to 20 per cent deteriorate, across the different therapeutic settings. In addition to that, a review of literature on alliance ruptures shows that they are far more frequent than therapists identify, or clients disclose (Muran, Safran, & Eubanks-Carter, 2010; Safran, Muran, & Eubanks-Carter, 2011).

Client preferences, their beliefs about psychotherapy, their role, and that of the therapist, have impact on therapeutic outcomes and dropouts (Auger, 2013), and it seems that therapeutic dialogues not just about what the client want to change, but their views, preferences and beliefs about the therapeutic process would need to form a part of the therapeutic dialogue and feedback, as suggested by Cooper and McLeod (2011) in their book on pluralistic psychotherapy.

This leads us to the question of how can we develop evaluation of our practice, and adapt some of the structured methods of feedback, whilst maintaining a reflexive therapeutic stance.

## Research summary

- Meta-analytic studies continue to confirm the general effectiveness in psychotherapy, although clinical guidelines still favour 'evidence-based treatments', based on single diagnoses and evidence from RCTs.
- Therapeutic relationship is one of the well-established aspects of the therapeutic process, with a good level of evidence for several aspects: therapeutic alliance, therapist responsiveness, empathy, agreement on goals and repair of ruptures.
- Clients are active participants in the therapeutic process and their agency, motivation, attachment styles, preferences, and levels of distress at entering psychotherapy, are linked to outcomes, as well as early termination.
- Therapists' effectiveness varies with individual clients and between therapists. Research highlights the importance of flexibility, openness, repair of ruptures and engagement in feedback.

## Using evaluation in psychotherapy practice

In this book, we have been making a case for a reflexive approach to clinical work, aiming to increase the quality of practice. Use of questionnaires can be devoid of reflection or therapeutic usefulness, as many practitioners who use them in statutory services have found. When this happens, questionnaires become an external requirement and a 'bit of admin' that ensures the provision of services, but the information is not used therapeutically. However, this type of evaluation gives scope for additional reflection and client engagement, particularly when therapists make agreements with clients about using them reflectively, and for meta-therapeutic dialogue.

## Evaluating reflectively

Evaluation is an important aspect of reflection-in-action (Schön, 1983) and allows a practitioner to recognise and reflect on their theories of action and make changes to their practice in order to meet clinical needs. Different methods of evaluation could help us to develop different forms of knowledge and add complexity to our understanding of clinical practice. In Chapter 6, we discussed different sources and types of knowledge that can be used in clinical practice. They have complementary functions and can be used to develop a multi-faceted view of what goes on within a therapeutic setting. Our methods of evaluation need to mirror that process. In the experience of using sessional questionnaires for Routine Outcomes Evaluation (ROE) within a relational community clinic, clients use questionnaires to take charge of their own process as well as give feedback to therapists. This is particularly the case when voicing issues they find difficult to broach such as suicidal ideation, or feeling misunderstood by the therapist. Therapists often use measures to gain a broader insight into changes in clients' distress and feedback. In using quantitative evaluation relationally, it is important to make an agreement with clients about how and when to use them, and how to reflect on the content and the process of completing them.

## Questionnaires

There is currently a range of questionnaires suitable for feedback and evaluation of clinical practice. Most of them are freely accessible and can be used by individual practitioners, as well as services. The following is just a brief, non-exclusive overview.

### Client preferences

Building on the research about therapist responsiveness, a new measure has been developed by Cooper and Norcross (Cooper & Norcross, 2016), which asks clients to rate their preferences in psychotherapy in terms of directiveness, emotional intensity, past or present orientation, focus on warm support or focused challenge. This type of meta-therapeutic dialogues is seen by the authors as a cornerstone of a pluralistic approach to therapy (Cooper & McLeod, 2011).

### Therapeutic relationship

Several measures could be used during therapy to give feedback on the working alliance: Working Alliance Inventory (Bordin, 1979; Tracey & Kokotovic, 1989), or broader questionnaires such as Session Rating Scale (Elliott, 1993; Miller, Duncan, & Johnson, 2002), or Helpful Aspects of Therapy (HAT) (Elliott, 1993), which combines qualitative feedback with a questionnaire format.

## Symptoms and problems

There are several questionnaires that can be used in assessment, as well during therapy, to give feedback on the changes in symptoms and problems. CORE Outcome questionnaires are designed for assessment of general distress and can be used in the long form of 34 questions (CORE 2007 Information Management Systems Ltd.), or as a short 10 questions measure (CORE Information Management Systems Ltd., 2007). Brief measures for depression, PHQ-9 (Kroenke, Spitzer, & Williams, 2001), and anxiety, GAD-7 (Spitzer, Kroenke, Williams, & Lowe, 2006), are also used in the NHS IAPT services (CSIP, 2008).

# Action research in evaluation

One of the challenges in evaluating the process of psychotherapy and counselling is linked to finding the methodology that can help us to understand what really happened, and develop a rich and informative source of knowledge, helpful to the client as well as the practitioner. The action research structure of reflection, action and evaluation can provide a useful structure for this type of evaluation, and use mixed methods of quantitative as well as qualitative evaluation.

# Research summary

## What methods can we use for evaluating our own practice?

*Quantitative evaluation*

This type of evaluation uses outcome questionnaires and measures. Practitioners are sometimes reluctant to use these methods for fear of adversely affecting the therapeutic relationship and anxiety about their own performance. However, research suggests that this type of evaluation offers clients an opportunity to give feedback to therapists and is shown to improve the therapeutic outcomes (Barkham, Mellor-Clark, & Stiles, 2015; Lambert, Whipple, & Kleinstäuber, 2018). Engaging clients in reflection on the content and process of completing questionnaires has a potential to add to the relational depth of the sessions and help to deal with ruptures.

*Qualitative evaluation*

The process of reflection-in-action can take place either within the session or after the session but during therapy. The therapist can use different forms of knowledge and their subjective experience in order to reflect on the process, recognise their theories of action and change them to meet the requirements of their practice, as explored in previous chapters. It can be helpful to develop a structure for this type of reflection, for example, using recording and sessional transcripts, IPR, learning journal and clinical supervision.

The following case study is an example of how you might use different types of evaluation to reflect on your practice.

## Case study 8.1

### Tunde and James

Tunde came to see James for counselling at the time when she was suffering from anxiety. She was entitled to a maximum of 12 sessions, paid for by her employer. She had been off sick for a month. Prior to this, she had had a panic attack most mornings before going to work. While she was off sick, she did not experience panic attacks but had nightmares about work filled with anxiety. In the initial assessment, James asked her about work and she told him that there had been conflicts in her team at work for the last six months. She didn't want to 'take sides' and tried to have a good working relationship with both her manager and colleagues. Both sides had become angry with her and started to shun her. Her manager started the procedure of monitoring her competency.

### Using quantitative analysis for reflection

James used Routine Outcomes Evaluation in his practice. Prior to assessment, he asked Tunde to complete the questionnaire about her preferences for therapy, using Cooper-Norcross Inventory of Preferences (Cooper & Norcross, 2016) as well as questionnaires for depression, PHQ-9 (Kroenke et al., 2001) and anxiety GAD-7 (Spitzer et al., 2006), and bring them to the first session. He told her that he would look at the questionnaires briefly at the start and then talk about them.

Tunde's responses showed that she was looking for a therapist who was directive, offered warm support and focused on the present. A score of over 15 on GAD-7 indicated severe anxiety. Her scores also indicated a major depressive episode and showed that she thought of hurting herself for at least half of the week.

Conversation about her questionnaires led to an exploration of her reasons for coming to therapy and James inquired further into her experience of anxiety. Through this, he came to understand that her depression related mostly to feelings of hopelessness about finding a way of dealing with her problems at work. He asked about her thoughts of self-harm. She explained that she had no plans to harm herself but found her circumstances so difficult that she often thought she would be 'better off dead'. She felt relieved that he asked about this, as it was something she didn't disclose to anyone else.

James used the results on the inventory of preferences to talk to Tunde about how they were going to work in therapy. They agreed that it was most important for her to focus on her problems at work and have space to express how she felt in the sessions. He asked about what she meant by wanting him to be directive and she said that she didn't want therapy to be 'just a chat' but wanted feedback, questions and techniques. This gave him an opportunity to talk about how he worked. He said that he did not usually give his own opinions or ask many questions because he saw therapy as a space where she would develop her own understanding and develop ways of dealing with them. However, he was happy to offer reflection and ask questions to deepen their dialogue and suggest some relaxation techniques if she found that helpful. He also added that he saw their therapeutic relationship as a part of therapy, and he was interested in hearing from her how she experienced their interactions, particularly the times when she felt he 'didn't get her'. She agreed with this. They arranged that she would complete the two questionnaires (GAD7 and PHQ-9) each week, bring them to the session, where he would look at them briefly at the start. They could go into them in more depth during the session, or not, depending on their mutual assessment. They also agreed to review their work every four sessions and that this would involve talking about how they worked together, and whether they needed to change anything.

### Using phenomenological reflection

Willis (1999) referred to using phenomenology in reflective practice by using three modes of reflection.

- *Contextual reflection* when therapists aim to uncover the social and cultural forces shaping the activity. In this case study, James was interested in the context and environment in which Tunde was working. He discovered that her organisation was going through a major period of change, resulting in a very stressful working environment. Tunde was the newest member of the team and scared of losing her job through redundancy. She was a single parent and a sole breadwinner. As a black woman, she had previous experiences of discrimination and did not expect good outcomes from the organisation. James was a white, middle-class male. He reflected on their difference and his relative privilege and was mindful of its relevance in their work.
- *Dispositional or self-reflection* refers to recognising one's own attitudes and beliefs. James has had an experience of being made redundant at work. This was something that helped him make a decision to change careers and become a counsellor. He was mindful that this was very different from Tunde's experience and her concerns and did not want to impose his expectations on her.
- During *experiential reflection*, practitioners contemplate practice as a lived experience by thinking back over what the event (or a session) was like as an experience. James recognised that he felt swamped by the amount of detail Tunde had given him in the session and wondered about what this meant. Did she feel she had to make sure she gave him the exact picture? Was she trying to make everything right? He was reminded of her trying to 'keep the peace' at work and decided to hold this as a possible theme for exploration. He used his theoretical background of Transactional Analysis to formulate this experience as an unconscious pattern, possibly stemming from her history.

*(Continued)*

## Comment

All of these areas of reflection helped James to begin to develop a treatment plan to help Tunde achieve her aims in therapy.

The process demonstrates the use of questionnaires in clinical practice and a cycle of reflective inquiry (experience and reflection leading to action), and a collaborative agreement of the initial aims and strategies:

- To help Tunde reduce the level of anxiety by teaching her some skills for relaxation and grounding;
- To reflect on the conflict at work and support her in developing strategies for dealing with conflict;
- To have a space to talk about her experiences of hopelessness and anxiety, and explore her expectations of herself and others;
- To jointly use the questionnaires to monitor changes from session to session.

These aims were then evaluated during their work together and led to gradual changes and adjustments. James worked for an employer assistance agency, and the questionnaires also had a purpose to demonstrate the effectiveness of their provision.

---

## Activity 8.1

It is suggested here that clients can use evaluation as another way of taking ownership of the therapeutic process and engagement between the sessions.

- Consider how could you use questionnaires in the therapeutic process. Which questionnaires would you use? How would you ensure you use them collaboratively with your clients?
- How could you use the questionnaires to deepen the reflection on the therapeutic process? Is there anything that would be particularly challenging for you? Perhaps there is a way you could include this type of client feedback into your supervision.

## A summary of the chapter

- Meta-analytic studies continue to confirm the general effectiveness in psychotherapy, although clinical guidelines still favour 'evidence-based treatments', based on single diagnoses and evidence from RCTs.
- Therapeutic relationship is one of the well-established aspects of the therapeutic process, with a good level of evidence for several aspects:

therapeutic alliance, therapist responsiveness, empathy, agreement on goals and repair of ruptures.

- Clients are active participants in the therapeutic process and engagement is linked to therapeutic outcomes.
- Therapists' effectiveness varies with individual clients and between therapists, and research evidence suggests a need for more feedback to counter a self-assessment bias.
- Combining questionnaires with cycles of reflection and inquiry into the therapeutic process can develop therapist responsiveness to client feedback and support client engagement.

# 9

# The vulnerable researcher

## Harnessing reflexivity for practice-based qualitative inquiry

### By Simon du Plock

> **Core knowledge**
>
> - This chapter brings us back to the subject of reflexivity and expands on what originally was referred to in terms of the essence of reflective practice as 'harnessing' the process towards transformative learning.
> - The chapter explores research with an interest in personal and professional development. It demystifies the term research and illustrates how research can move from naïve to systematic inquiry.

We have paid attention, so far, to how reflexivity can enrich our clinical therapeutic work. I want now to encourage you to think about the contribution reflexivity can make to our research activities. In doing so, I want to go beyond 'talking the talk' towards 'walking the talk' – by which I mean that I will pursue my line of argument by providing an example of my own research. In doing so, I hope to demonstrate the impact of this strategy on both the prime researcher (in this instance myself) and participants/co-researchers.

Therapists who take reflexivity seriously are ideally positioned to generate forms of research grounded in first-person experience and naive inquiry.

I will outline the preliminary stages of such research to illustrate how this subjective experience and the specific research trajectory it entails provide a source of thick description and hypothesis that may be explored further with co-researchers.

## Researching the experience of illness

The early stages of such an inquiry are not dissimilar to the process of reflection and analysis to be found in the practice of humanistic (and especially existential) therapy. The particular study I will use as my vehicle for discussing reflexivity in research suggests that diagnosis of a chronic illness may precipitate a profound shift in identity that can be exacerbated or engaged with creatively according to the differing relational styles adopted by health-care professionals. I hope you will be able to see the ways in which being (or at least striving to become) an explicitly reflexive researcher provided me with insights and rich descriptive material that would not otherwise have surfaced. I include a number of exercises that I hope will prompt you in your own reflexive journey in relation to your sense of self as an inquirer/researcher.

## Demystifying the notion of 'research'

I have argued (du Plock, 2004) that we therapists are in a fortunate position with regard to research. When we are confronted with research, we are ourselves primarily researchers in our everyday activity as we go about our business of providing therapy. As McLeod points out, we are constantly engaged in 'research' as we go through life and in our clinical work:

> A counselling session with a client can be seen as a piece of research, a piecing together of information and understandings, followed by testing the validity of conclusions and actions based on shared knowing ...

> A useful working definition of research is: a systematic process of critical inquiry leading to valid propositions and conclusions that are communicated to interested others. (McLeod, 1994: 4)

We get into difficulties, it seems to me, when we forget this and begin to see research as something different and separate from what we are already intimately involved in.

As an aid to reflection, I find it helpful to ask myself, 'Where am I with research?' In prompting myself in this way, I am making use of my existential-therapy training, and I am thinking of Rollo May's observation in *Existence* (May et al., 1979) that where we are in terms of our relational world is often a more useful question than how we feel. So if I follow this guidance, I can ask myself, 'Am I even in the room with research?' and 'What do I mean when I use the word anyway?'

## Intimidating concept

The word 'research' itself can feel intimidating: if you are not a graduate, then you may believe (erroneously, I think) that you are a stranger to research; if you have an arts degree, you may feel estranged from the sorts of 'scientific' research increasingly required in the therapy field. Perhaps worst of all, if you have a psychology degree, you may have found yourself working with statistical models and computer packages that seem to deliver little of direct relevance to your understanding of the human condition. I recall in my own psychology undergraduate degree that the emphasis was on the generation of statistically significant findings – and 'human being' was obscured beneath a concern with observable, measurable behaviour. There is nothing essentially wrong with this, of course, especially given that undergraduate psychology is not primarily concerned with therapy, but in the absence of careful reflection it is easy to invest research with past meanings and fail to see its present possibilities. One response to the anxiety to which the notion of research can give rise is to simply reject it as a valid enterprise – in the face of the 'otherness' of research we may defensively say it is 'not what we do'.

## Research summary

If I am to take reflexivity seriously, I need to ask myself whether it is something that I do. In engaging with, rather than distancing myself from, research, I notice once more the relevance of a therapeutic approach to this question. It is interesting to recall the formulaic intervention, 'I wonder what you mean when you say x?' While it is to be hoped that our interventions vary in tune with client material, this still seems to be a useful question and, like most useful questions, it is worthwhile asking it of ourselves. So if I ask myself, 'When do I think I am doing research?', I find I respond with a large number of examples including the following:

- A trainee asks me whether I can suggest any literature on x, a topic for which they have been unable to locate any texts.
- I am invited to facilitate an 'away-day' for a group of clinical psychologists wanting to reassess their professional goals.
- I reflect (or self-analyse) on an aspect of a therapy session and refer to a paper on this aspect to help me explore further.
- I read about dementia after a relative has been diagnosed with the condition.
- I take an issue from therapeutic work to peer supervision.
- I am prompted by the lack of published material on similarities between existential therapy and cognitive–analytic therapy to write a paper that attempts to address this gap.

While, typically, only the last of these examples would be considered to constitute research as it is generally defined, I think that each provides an example of a form of research when this is considered more broadly and creatively. Each calls me into a particular engagement with the world, one that is characterised by an attempt to explore and make new connections between aspects of this world. Clearly these activities are distinct from the kind of carefully controlled laboratory-style experiments that are designed to fit the criteria of reliability, validity and generalisability (two, at least, might also be viewed as therapy or self-development). Nor are they similar to the observational studies, case studies or surveys and questionnaires that researchers often employ. Perhaps these activities might be termed 'inquiry' rather than research, as I am, in each instance, enquiring about my world.

In this regard, I am reminded of the model of the person as a problem-solving investigator of their world. In this sense I would want to argue that the sort of inquiry of which this chapter is a product should count as research.

## Activity 9.1

This exercise is designed to help you begin thinking about the ways you use the notion of research, and the extent to which these are examples of 'accepted wisdom' or reflect the needs of your own personal and professional journey. You might undertake this exercise individually, or by working in pairs.

- If working individually, write down what comes to mind when you ask your-self the questions: 'When do I do research?' and 'How do I know when I am doing research, and not some other activity?'
- If working in pairs, you might take turns to speak while your colleague scribes for you. When you have generated a response to these questions, take some time to reflect on these, either individually or in dialogue. In particular, notice how you feel about your responses, and whether you would like these responses to be different in some regard.

## Researching illness

Two significant life events – being diagnosed in late 2006 as having myalgic encephalomyelitis (ME/CFS) and the opportunity in 2007 to lead a research (as against a professional) doctorate – have encouraged me to think more deeply about the nature of inquiry. (I shall use 'inquiry' and 'research' interchangeably in this chapter.) Both these events have added substance to my assertion that the researcher's identity – their sense of who they are – is as crucial a factor in what they can illumine as it is in the practice of psychotherapy. The notion of the neutral, objective researcher is as absurd as the notion of the neutral, objective therapist. In both cases the illumination they can provide depends upon who they are – or perhaps where they are – in relation to either the client or the topic of research. I find it helpful to conceptualise this 'whereness' in terms of 'research trajectory', by which I mean the angle at which the researcher enters into an explorative process. The angle at which we enter any field of inquiry determines what is illuminated, and also what is thrown into shadow. I say 'thrown into shadow' because there is neither light nor shadow prior to the advent of the inquirer. As this trajectory serves to privilege some aspects of the phenomenon under consideration, and obscure others, it is important for us to be aware of our subjective stance at the outset of the research.

Rejecting the possibility of being a neutral investigator, I need to describe clearly my own research trajectory in relation to the experience of being diagnosed with a chronic illness. In some respects, I am attempting no more than to take seriously the axiom of existential–phenomenological investigation that the 'co-researcher', a term used to indicate the co-constructedness of 'reality' entailed in both therapy and research, should pay appropriate attention to the meanings they bring to the phenomenon under consideration.

## Reflection

Ruth Behar (1996: 13), writing about 'humanistic anthropology', makes clear that researchers who locate themselves in their own texts forfeit the defensive position of 'scientific observer':

> Writing vulnerability takes as much skill, nuance, and willingness to follow through on all the ramifications of a complicated idea as does writing invulnerably and distantly. I would say it takes yet greater skill … To assert that one is a 'white middle-class woman' or a 'black gay man' or a 'working-class Latina' … is only interesting if one is able to draw deeper connections between one's personal experience and the subject under study. That doesn't require a full-length autobiography, but it does require a keen understanding of what aspects of the self are the most important filters through which one perceives the world and, more particularly, the topic being studied.

I find Behar's words resonate very strongly with me, and it is for this reason that I have included the notion of 'the vulnerable researcher' in the title of this chapter.

## Activity 9.2

What comes up for you when you read Behar's words? This exercise is designed to help you begin thinking about what you invest in research, and what it might be like for you to include yourself within your research in appropriate ways.

This exercise is best undertaken in pairs. Take turns to pose the following questions to each other:

- Who do I think I am when I say I am a researcher?
- What does this sense of self as a researcher include, and what does it exclude?
- What might it be like to expand what is included within this notion of researcher?
- What would be the advantages of expanding this notion?
- What do you think some of the costs might be?

When you have generated a response to these questions, take some time to reflect on these. In particular, notice how you feel about your responses, and whether you would like these responses to be different in some regard.

## Change of professional identity

The *raison d'être* of the Doctorate in Psychotherapy jointly offered by Metanoia Institute and Middlesex University is the promotion of research by fully qualified therapists that emerges out of their clinical and professional practice and that makes a distinct contribution to the scholarly community of therapists. My role in relation to the Doctorate has given me the chance to take forward ideas that I had expressed some years earlier:

> We need to take more seriously the idea of research as a personal journey of discovery, or perhaps re-search, a continual transformation process rather than a discrete event. Research must not, of course, remain only of personal significance if it is to have any impact on professional practice – it must be disseminated, and evaluated by our peers, colleagues, and clients. (du Plock, 2004: 32)

The researcher–practitioner is at the heart of this activity, since it is they who reflect on their work to identify what is needful, and they who at every stage of the research are required to engage with others in their specialist field to ensure the relevance of their work. This researcher–practitioner ethos is underlined by the requirement that their activities not only are conducted at doctoral level (i.e., can be mapped on to an agreed set of doctoral descriptors) but also generate a 'product' – a specific innovation in the form of a text, training programme, new research tool, etc. – that 'makes a difference' to clinical practice. This ethos is congruent with my own conceptualisation of the inquirer as the central, reflexive focus of the activity.

## Reflection

If we are to take this notion of the researcher's role to heart, we need to know about the journey they have taken to generate their product. An account of the

*(Continued)*

research journey may provide information as significant as anything encapsulated in the formal outcome of the inquiry. It also evidences via thick description their research trajectory, and in doing so enhances the validity of the inquiry. It makes no more sense to think about objective inquiry as separate from the researcher than it does to think about the client isolated from the therapist – each co-constitutes the other.

## Change of personal identity

The impact of the experience of illness on sense of self and identity has received considerable attention, particularly from the symbolic interactionist perspective (Bury, 1991; Charmaz, 1983; Corbin & Strauss, 1987). A number of writers have used their findings to explore the specific problems presented by chronic illness, including chronic fatigue syndrome (Clark & James, 2003). My diagnosis as having ME presented me with a radical challenge to my sense of identity in a number of ways, some of which are relevant here. Diagnosis typically entails an 'expert' of some kind making a judgement about another person who, generally, is considered a 'non-expert'. In medical terms, a doctor tells their patient that they 'have' a certain illness or condition. When the patient is a psychologist and the condition one generally thought to be at least partly psychosomatic in nature, the authority and power in play become complex and problematic. This is perhaps particularly so given the existential–phenomenological critiques of diagnosis with which I became familiar in the course of my own therapy training. It may also be that my previous way of constructing a sense of self heightened the challenge of this diagnosis. As Aujoulat, Luminet and Deccache argue in their research into the experience of chronic illness:

> People who had previously enjoyed being in control of things and who described themselves as having a managerial type of personality appeared in our study to be at greater risk of experiencing a feeling of loss of their sense of identity. (Aujoulat, Luminet, & Deccache, 2007: 9)

I found myself thrown into a process of inquiry in which I was not merely the prime researcher but also the primary subject, as I sought to engage with questions such as: 'How do I feel about "having" an illness?' 'How might ME impact on my sense of identity?' 'What does it mean to be a psychotherapist with a chronic debilitating condition?' As a psychologist I found it natural to reflect on this challenge by reading in depth about ME and keeping a diary to structure what at least initially seemed a situation over which I could exercise little control.

## Helicopter view

At the outset I did not specifically frame as research the literature search I undertook or the diary in which I recorded my subjective experience both of the condition and of my interaction with healthcare professionals. When I rose above the situation to take a helicopter view, I conceptualised them as subjective strategies adopted in response to a personal situation. In the case of diary-keeping, I was informed by my knowledge of the therapeutic effects of writing structured accounts of stressful experiences (Hunt, 2000; Hunt & Sampson, 2002; Pennebaker, 1993; Philips, Penman, & Linnington, 1999). I soon noted, though, that I found both activities therapeutically useful, and I began to make connections between this insight and my existing professional knowledge. As an example, I visited NHS and other websites on ME and chronic fatigue syndrome (CFS) after my diagnosis and felt reassured to discover how precisely the label mapped my symptoms, even though they invariably emphasised the limitations of the few available treatments. This reminded me how therapy clients often seek a label for their condition and can be dismayed rather than relieved when therapists cannot or will not provide one. Similarly, I found I kept increasingly detailed verbatim accounts of my meetings with healthcare professionals. Writing these records assisted me in de-briefing; it also helped me to obtain an enhanced sense of mastery, as I was able to identify their different relational styles.

## From naïve to systematic inquiry

This movement from subjective experience towards more general (I would not say objective) experience meant that soon my idiosyncratic questions were re-framed as:

- What does it mean to 'have' an illness?
- How might a diagnosis of ME impact upon sense of identity?
- What is it like for a psychotherapist to be diagnosed with a possibly psychosomatic condition?

I found relatively little had been written – or at least published – addressing these questions. This led me to further hypothesise the following:

- There is something about the identity of 'psychotherapist' that makes it difficult for us to engage with our own experience of illness.

In this connection I noted that Bayne in *The needs of counsellors and psychotherapists* (cited in Varma, 1997), writes about emotional self-care, though primarily in terms of using strategies to cope with stress.

Without necessarily doing so in full awareness, I found I had taken my diagnosis and actively sought to understand it as 'a continual transformation process' with which I developed a close relationship, rather than accepting it passively as a victim. I also found paradoxically that in closing with it to make it my own, my inquiry became one of more than just personal significance. In the wider inquiry that I undertook, and that I plan to write up for future publication, I found I journeyed from a descriptive self-analysis of the type with which phenomenological inquiry can open to a consideration of the co-constitution of relationship in the course of professional consultation.

## Moving from naive inquiry to research

In the process above, I moved from naive inquiry – the acquiring of information which we do on a daily basis – towards research/inquiry. In distinguishing between naive inquiry and research, Barber says:

> to qualify as research, your inquiry must involve a careful searching, your method of collecting information must be located within a recognizable methodological tradition, and you must demonstrate systematic investigation and critical reflection upon both what you are doing and how you are doing it. You need also to illuminate your motivation and rationale and what influences you at the time. (Barber, 2006: 89)

## Recording reflectively

The diary in which I recorded accounts of my meetings with each of the health professionals involved in my treatment provided a way of keeping track of this complex process, since five professionals played a role: two general practitioners, a practice nurse, a medical herbalist and a clinical psychologist. While my thinking was that maintaining a record would allow me to 'stay in the driving seat' in a pragmatic sense, I soon noticed that writing functioned as a way of de-briefing. I moved from recording primarily factual information to a more comprehensive reflection on my feelings prior to, during and following each meeting. I found that I looked forward to meetings with the clinical psychologist and medical herbalist, even though both entailed a fatiguing journey of several miles. In contrast, I generally felt apprehensive about my meetings with the GPs and practice nurse, even though the surgery was a short walk from my home. I also noticed that I wrote verbatim notes after visits to the GP surgery, while I often recorded only a summary of meetings with the psychologist and herbalist. This structured inquiry had clear therapeutic functions for me in helping me to make distress and confusion meaningful.

### Activity 9.3

I agree with Sousa (2007) when he argues that therapy and research should not be conflated; I would also suggest that, while it is often important to conceptualise them as distinct activities, research can be therapeutic, and therapy involves exploration akin to research.

Reflect on the following in pairs:

- Think about ways in which you seek to engage with difficult or challenging events in your own life.

Do they share any similarities with the strategies I have described? Perhaps they are very different? To what extent do they enable you to generate new perspectives on and wisdom about an aspect of living? Do these ways of being relate in some ways to how you think about the world when you are being a researcher?

## The emergence of an organising theme: 'openness to relationship'

Within the first month of treatment, the theme of 'relationship' surfaced to link my observations. As an existential–phenomenological therapist I am constantly aware of ways in which I can hold myself open to, or close down, the possibilities of being-with-the-client. I know that a number of factors are involved in this, including my willingness, or otherwise, to hold myself open for the experience that May, Angel, & Ellenberger (1979) describe as the experience of 'here-is-a-new-person'. Our ability to encounter the other in this open manner is a prerequisite according to May et al. for the other to have an 'I-am' experience. While I have sometimes become aware of the I-am experience as a therapy client I had not previously had this experience within a relatively short time of working as a client with five different healthcare professionals. I found it instructive and illuminating to reflect on the ways in which each embodied a relational style that, to some extent, determined their availability for relationship. These reflections became a major organising theme in my research diary. Typically (and I had numerous meetings with these five professionals), I found I felt less unwell after meetings with the herbalist and psychologist. The herbalist, medically trained but without a counselling background, tended to present as interested and available for encounter. Briefly, her focus was holistic (she would ask me open questions about myself, and discuss various options and recent research in a relatively equal way, free of jargon). She did not attempt to hide herself but, equally, did not disclose inappropriately. She presented smartly but relatively informally in terms of dress, and sat to the side of her desk while taking notes. I found it interesting and reassuring that she was transparent in this way, permitting me, for instance, to follow her train of thought when she was considering various prescriptions. Appointments were for 30 minutes but often extended to 40 minutes. Her boundaries were flexible but holding. My sense was that she was available but kept secure boundaries. Reflecting on this, I felt that her style of engagement was broadly similar to that to which I aspire in my own clinical work.

I found that my therapist, an experienced male clinical psychologist in his early or mid-forties, was generally open to a relationship based on mutual understanding. It was disarming, especially as an existential practitioner, to be greeted at our first appointment by 'I've Googled you, and I feel I know you already!' My response 'Well, I've done the same to see what you've published' left us in a curious position. I think our mutual agreement that we would need to start from scratch to think about what work we might undertake together was, in the event, helpful and supportive. Perhaps the most helpful aspect of our meetings was that he resonated with my frustration with the shortcomings of the general practitioners and supported my referral to a specialist clinic. I noticed that I looked forward to our meetings and did not need to use my diary to de-brief to the extent that I did after visiting the GP surgery.

In contrast, the female nurse there made little eye contact and was concerned to take blood samples as quickly and efficiently as possible. She disclosed nothing of herself or her training, and her mode of relationship was of the 'doing-to' type. Frustrated at our first meeting that I admitted a fear of needles, she responded, 'You're my second needle-phobic so far this morning – it's not my day!' Perhaps unsurprisingly I felt 'unseen' in these encounters, except insofar as I fitted the category of 'difficult patient'. The senior of the two general practitioners, a middle-aged man, stayed behind his desk most of the time and kept his eyes on a computer screen. His mode of relationship was to use the computer as intermediary. Having typed information into it, he would share the 'factual' information it generated. One of his most puzzling announcements was, 'How would it strike you if I told you that you have a 20 per cent chance of a heart attack in the next ten years?' I found this style of relating to me as if I were an audience for medical technology alienating; not only did I not feel seen, I felt that I had somehow failed to appreciate appropriately the technology with which the doctor was clearly enamoured. His colleague, a younger man perhaps in his late thirties, took pains to demonstrate his willingness to treat me as an equal by maintaining constant eye contact. So relentless was this that I began to fantasise that he had taken a short course in advanced empathy techniques. He explained in some detail what was known about ME. He seemed to thus invite my compliance with a long-term anti-depressant drug prescription and was baffled and defensive about what to suggest beyond this when I indicated I was not willing to take this route. While he agreed to refer me to a specialist clinic, he did so with the caution, 'A lot of people expect a cure but there isn't one.' As I had explicitly stated that I was seeking ways of managing a chronic condition, this seemed to indicate that, regardless of the amount of eye contact, once again I had not been seen but had been categorised as one among 'a lot of people'. Moreover, this category 'a lot of people' was clearly viewed as problematic.

## Activity 9.4

My experience, while I frame it in the context of being 'seen' by the other, reflects the findings of studies that have focused on patients' sense of self-determination and power. Such studies indicate that the key features of an empowering patient–medical practitioner relationship include continuity, patient-centredness, mutual acknowledgement and relatedness (Chang, Li, & Liu, 2004; McWilliam et al., 1996; Paterson, 2001). McWilliam et al. (1996) found that patients experienced empowerment in the process of telling their story if the healthcare professional is able to facilitate a mutual exploration of their situation and situatedness. In doing so, they argue that patient and practitioner collaborate to add or create meaning to the patient's experience. In contrast, Paterson (2001) finds that where the healthcare professional discounts experiential knowledge and provides inadequate resources, particularly in terms of time and continuity, the patient is likely to feel disempowered.

- Try to recall something from your own life – a negative experience where you continue to have strong emotions works best in this context. Relate it to your colleague.
- As you do so, notice how you tell your story. Do you organise the material in such a way as to reinforce an existing perspective that frames you in a particular role?
- Can you begin to think about ways of telling the story that might re-frame the material and make it more meaningful? Does the extent to which you feel 'heard' by your colleague assist you in such a re-framing?

## 'Relationship' re-framed in the context of the inquiry

Up to this point my observations were focused on the extent to which each healthcare professional was able to be in a relationship with me, according to my sense as an existential–phenomenological therapist of what the phenomenon of relationship might mean. I had noted how I felt more or less ill according to the extent to which each was able to encounter me. My thinking was increasingly that there might be a link between the experience of being 'seen' and feeling ill. As Charon asserts:

> The healing process begins when patients tell of symptoms or even fears of illness … These narratives, or pathographics as they are sometimes called, demonstrate how critical is the telling of pain and suffering, enabling patients to give voice to what they endure and to frame the illness so as to escape dominion by it. Without the narrative acts of telling and being heard, the patient cannot convey to anyone else – or to the self – what he or she is going through. More radically, and perhaps equally true, without these narrative acts, the patient cannot himself or herself grasp what the events of the illness mean. (Charon, 2006: 65, 66)

As the inquiry widened, a further cycle of research evolved – I began to think about these communication difficulties more systemically as it seemed to me that the various healthcare professionals were not able to hear each other. My impression was reinforced by the wording of the King's College Chronic Fatigue (CFS) Research and Treatment Unit website, where I found a cautionary note for prospective patients:

> The perpetual battle for validation that most sufferers of CFS are caught in is literally, physiologically exhausting, depressing and dispiriting. It affects the course of the illness. No other sufferer of chronic disease has to fight this bizarre battle to have the facts that they live with every day legitimized by a hostile authority. As long as CFS has to prove itself, that much longer will sufferers suffer. As therapists, our first and last concern is to take the suffering of clients seriously. All this involves is listening. (Deary, 2007)

While the message seems to be directed towards patients, it is obvious that such a 'battle for validation' is primarily one between the healthcare professionals themselves. As the website expresses it:

> Some GPs are sceptical about the existence or treatment of CFS/ME. If you are having problems getting a referral for these reasons, you could perhaps try another GP in your practice. (Deary, 2007)

The casual wording belies a serious problem: such a request will probably be interpreted as a challenge to the power structures of many GP practices. A healthy person might find making such a request daunting, and it is likely to exacerbate the symptoms experienced by an ME sufferer.

## Conclusion

To summarise the journey I have taken, I have – however briefly and sketchily – suggested that reflexivity enables therapists to ground their research in subjective experience and naive inquiry with confidence. My own personal and professional experiences have led me to an enhanced awareness of the 'self' of the researcher at the core of a reflexive process. A wealth of thick description of a phenomenon surfaces when we attend to the researcher's individual journey into the field. The thick description obtained at this early stage in the research journey provides a resource for reflection on later stages of inquiry. My own experience of a diagnostic process was the catalyst for personal identity questions and therapeutic activities that led to more general inquiry and the emergence of an organising theme – in this particular instance, that of health professionals' openness to being in relationship with the patient. This, in turn, led me to hypothesise about their openness to be in relation with each other, and the implications of systemic communication patterns for the patient's sense of self. While it is not always the case that the researcher is prompted by direct personal experience to embark on their inquiry, the resulting study is impoverished and, I would argue, less valid and trustworthy if the self of the researcher is excluded from their research journey.

# 10

# How creative writing aids our professional transition

## By Jeannie Wright

---

**Core knowledge**

This chapter revolves around life transitions:

- We will explore reflective writing, individually and collaborative, to make sense of life changes – personally and professionally.

---

## Making sense of the messiness of life

Jubilation – the warm bathwater of working life slowly ebbing away

The Spanish word for retirement is 'jubilacion'. A friend, who has moved between professional and manual jobs all her life, what she calls 'working with my body' or not, is about to retire and is holding a party to celebrate. Jubilacion, she says

> For me retirement from teaching is not quite so straightforward. There have been times in my working life when such a major shift would not have caused me such anxieties. What is a given is that I'll write my way through any transition.

For over five years, since thinking about giving up a full-time job, I've written in all kinds of places and forms about what the decision to leave paid work means. This chapter presents some of that writing. It also encourages you to do your own writing as reflection, or reflection in writing, and to read and re-read. It will help clarify, embolden, contain and a whole lot else, and the only way to know that is by doing it.

The warm bathwater of working life slowly ebbing away.

Recently I went to someone else's creative writing workshop, a real treat not to be there at the front. The facilitator was great, gave a clear guideline and then left us to get on with our writing. The instruction was to write a letter to our future selves. I can often write what I can't say – started young and have developed the habit. Some of the material for this chapter is therefore drawn from this personal writing; 'journalling' is not quite right, although there is now a substantial literature about regular expressive writing as journaling, and as a therapeutic tool (Bolton, 2011; Thompson & Adams, 2015).

At the workshop I found myself stuck, staring into space. It's not often I sit down with a pencil in my hand and no words arrive but this time – unusually – the writing just wouldn't come. Nothing wrong with staring into space, but I wanted to come away with something to re-read so I started with a list, that simplest and least threatening form of writing. The list was in answer to a question: What would I miss if I retired? 'Identity, the printer, working with some of the students, status, some of my colleagues, structure, IT Services, some of the students, talking about ideas, a sense of purpose and routine, an income. Did I mention the printer?' Out of that list came metaphors, looking up at me out of the depths. You can't force them. (For some joyful and often metaphorical tweets, look at Ian McMillan's morning strolls on Twitter @IMcmillan.) So, I came away with a list and some word pictures comparing things that are not alike, e.g., warm bath water and working life. This was not what our facilitator had suggested, and it didn't matter at all. Nobody was going to read what I'd written but me.

The metaphor in the sub-title above, 'the warm bathwater of working life slowly ebbing away' is an example of showing, not telling. One purpose of this chapter is to draw attention to the value of creative writing tools, such as images and metaphors, as part of reflective strategies. Images in creative writing can help us to connect with feelings that we are not consciously aware of, connect too with parts of ourselves. I wasn't fully aware of how important – and at times comforting – paid work has been in my life until that metaphor of the warm bathwater emerged. If and when you choose to show your writing to others, those same images can connect your thoughts and feelings with other people's too. More of this to come.

Of course, choosing to leave paid work is a privilege. For Tony, the (fictional) taxi driver in the dialogue below, choice has been very limited. Dialogue is a more extended form of creative writing and in this example introduces some of the tensions for people who are ageing and dealing with externally imposed upheavals in their working lives. Tony, now a taxi driver (who was an engineer), asks me, 'What do you do?'

He waits while I struggle with the seatbelt with arthritic fingers, an older male driving an older female. He has picked me up from a UK university residence with a suitcase, so he knows I have some connection with the university. There's a pause. I decide on, 'I teach.'

We move on to the fog forecast and then, watching the hard hats and steel-toe-capped builders arrive at the site across from where I live. There's another pause. I forego silence. 'This place employs a lot of people,' I say and he's off. He was 'retired' from production engineering after a takeover. Tony: 'This town used to be everything engineering, now the university must be the biggest employer, or maybe the hospital. Can't imagine a more pathetic job than driving. The one good thing about it is I go home when I like, get up when I like.' The light is red. We turn into the one scenic drive in this battered and historically carpet-bombed city. The road is suddenly tree-lined and curves down to the station. Me: 'With your qualifications and experience, it seems a waste. You could be passing on your knowledge.' Am I being deliberately provocative? The back of his neck straightens, Tony: 'Well, of course I applied for technician jobs. I thought they'd have my name written on them. No response from any of them. Even when I stopped putting my date of birth on applications. The only reason I got on to this was through an argument. Down at the dole, they started saying I'd got to take shelf stacking. I snatched the card up from the desk, "Right, I'll go for this!" And it was training to drive taxis, if you can call it training. There's no holiday pay and of course, when you don't have a company car, sick pay, pension – that's when you realise what you had.' He's angry and I estimate I may be another five minutes sitting in the back of this car. Tony carries on talking about what he misses from his previous engineering life, and how he only has a year to go before retirement proper, that is collecting his pension. We're now in a bowl of fog, then up and out into the sun outside the station. Tony: 'Do you want a receipt?' I imagine the invoice, 20 min counselling, or is it biographical or ethnographic research? He has told his story and been heard. He may feel valued, or may not. Other passengers may have taken the other seat, telling their stories, not listening to the driver's.

## Writing selves

Self-writing as part of reflection takes many forms, starting with lists (Bolton, Field, & Thompson, 2006). Many people baulk at the idea of writing because they carry the old shame of school, and being told they can't write, but everyone writes lists. I've already included the list of what I'd miss about paid work and here's another list of what I do enjoy about stopping paid work: space in the day to stare at trees, getting up when I feel like it, spontaneous walks, visits with friends, and sitting outside when the sun is shining. Lists are deceptively simple.

Some people have brought examples of their writing to our work together and we've used them to add to the talking in therapy and in supervision. The forms of that writing vary and all aid creative reflection. For example:

- Unsent letters/emails;
- Song lyrics;
- Poems on stones;
- Dream journals;
- Dialogues with other people or with parts of self.

Using fictional characters, such as Tony and Leslie, who will both appear in this chapter, is a way of distancing, and allows more freedom of expression, especially if there is traumatic memory in the experience (Etherington, 2003). Tony and Leslie are fictional in the sense that they have emerged from my imagination, and also reflect my experience and relationships, of course. This is an ethical as well as creative decision. No story is ever about only one person, the one called the writer (Tullis, 2013). The ethics of personal and fictional writing as published narrative research, similar to those of writing autoethnographies, are fraught and will be returned to (Josselson, 2011; Wyatt & Adams, 2014).

There is a long tradition of using creative writing in career, health and therapeutic settings and an increasing research literature (Lengelle & Meijers, 2014; Williamson & Wright, 2018). This chapter will signpost some of that research. Its aim is also to suggest you try out some writing activities, so if you haven't got a screen, keyboard or paper and pen to hand, now's the time to get them. Crayons, felt-tips, pencil? It doesn't matter. Whatever you feel most at ease with.

## Unsent letters/emails

The unsent letter, now more likely to be an email or tweet, is a familiar therapeutic writing tool. It's crucial that the writer chooses whether to press send, or not. Here's an example of an unsent email from Leslie, who's about to leave the world of academia:

> Dear students and colleagues,
>
> I'm taking my mono-functional equipment (a clock) and leaving you to it. Updating the yellowing handouts? Yes, I can see the need for that, but becoming part of an entertainment industry on social media? No. Updating Twitter every time I turn round because Marketing says so? No. Hot desking? Good luck with that.
>
> All the best Leslie – the grey-haired one who used to teach you .... (Enter a subject as desired)

Leslie's rant, to former students and colleagues, expresses hurt. For some, leaving paid work is forced; they would prefer to stay in the workplace, possibly even to die in harness. Leslie is ambivalent. She writes in a journal entry:

> I'm very tired and fed up. The work just irritates me now. I don't really want to do it anymore, especially in this newly 'students as consumers' environment. It pays though, and sometimes does that thing of distracting: work as anaesthesia. I suppose I'll have to find other painkillers.

In the UK, at last count, three quarters of people aged over 50 are still in work and 1 in 8 people aged over 65 are still in the paid work force and that figure is likely to go up. Encouraged by governmental policies, staying in paid work for people between the ages of 50 and 74 is a growing area of opportunity (Office for National Statistics, https://www.gov.uk/government/news/employ ment-minister-calls-on-businesses-tocreate-more-opportunities-for-older-workers). However, being the oldest in your workplace 'they're young enough to be my grandchildren' is not always a comfortable place to be.

Wherever or whatever you've been able to hang this life around, you're suddenly, like your Skoda in the works car park, the oldest on the corridor. The departmental mug shots show rows of youthful and middle-aged faces. You're elderly, a crone and a half. And there's not much of the 'elder' in terms of respect when reflecting on feeling elderly in this particular workplace.

Shaming is the organisational leverage that pushes many out. Based on experience of retirees and those about to leave paid work in wealthier parts of the world, I'm conscious of how gender and social class impact on retirement stories. So why is Leslie so resistant to the idea of more leisure time?

> It's the day of the leaving do. I have specifically asked not to have one, and feel relieved that it's partly diluted by two others moving on from this workplace. It's outside too – not in some cramped corridor, with bought cakes and some colleagues looking anxiously at their phones in case they're missing an email/Tweet/Facebook post. The genial Head of Department makes jokes and refers to me as 'retiring'. That's not what I'm about to do. However, he seems unable to accept that I'm going to get another job, and definitely not about to set off on a Saga cruise. 'All the best, Leslie,' he says. We all smile, drink the warm wine and go back to work.

One of the major strengths of the kind of creative writing illustrated here is the freedom to express thoughts and feelings openly, anywhere and with any kind of equipment, from the pencil and back of anything that's write-able on, to the tablet/phone/laptop. The privacy of this first write is essential. There is no audience, no judge, no critic (Wright, 2018).

## Activity 10.1

### Your future self

This is an opportunity to spend 10 minutes writing about your future self. Write without self-criticism, or at least turn down the volume on the inner critic. What do you want? What don't you want? Nobody will see this writing but you.

When you have written for about the 10 mins suggested, see how it's going. If you've done, read what you've written.

NB Safeguard your writing! Store it carefully if you want to re-read, or delete/shred destroy it if not.

## Autoethnography, writing as inquiry and ethics

The creative traditions and colours of writing for reflection run into approaches to research where writing about personal experience is honoured, such as in autoethnography and writing as inquiry (Richardson & St Pierre, 2005). One of the differences is that the 'product' of the writing is more dominant, rather than the writing process. For example, during transitions between jobs and between countries, for me, personal writing is anchoring and the reflection it affords in re-reading is full of insight (Wright, 2009). The jump from personal and therapeutic (this writing is for my eyes only) to producing writing within a cultural and political envelope for publication has hazy boundaries: it helps me to understand the experience from a wider angle; it may also connect with others' experience and it raises complex ethical issues.

'Autoethnography is a way of caring for the self' (Adams, Holman Jones, & Ellis, 2015: 62). Is it? There is a kind of protection in writing, and paradoxically, deciding to publish that intimate, autoethnographic writing is also a risky way to share vulnerabilities (Wright, 2003). Once the given audience is invited in, there's no way of taking back the invitation, and the occasional need to 'speak' to a wider audience leaves me feeling exposed, and not just about me, but also about the other people who are inevitably woven into the parts of my life I choose to write about.

Most of my writing goes into cupboards or in bags under beds. Ethically, that is a much safer option. Those writings have done their job as a kind of therapy; they have no need to go anywhere else – it's a private outpouring and not for anyone else's eyes. Do the unique and emotionally powerful insights of autoethnographic accounts make it worth the anguish of risking publication? Sometimes. As an approach to research, this is still contested ground. And, as some of the leaders in the field argue, it's worth the anguish involved in publishing because of the possible connections with other people; that personal story might do some 'good in the world'.

Certainly, finding autoethnographer Ron Pelias' evocative writing about the indecision facing him at the end of an academic career made me smile (Pelias, 2015). Hanging on, or letting go, I felt he understood my dilemma as I read about his. As Tony Adams says in a film by Kitrina Douglas about autoethnography, 'I can write about homophobia in my life in ways that no interviewer could ever capture' (Douglas & Carless, 2016).

Autoethnography is a useful part of the repertoire of social science research, and links creative writing and reflection, but is not for the faint-hearted. Your personal thoughts and feelings, once in print, cannot be changed or taken back (Holman Jones, Adams, & Ellis, 2013; Wyatt & Adams, 2014).

## Writing poetry and song lyrics

Poetry is a 'hotline to the heart' in poet Andrew Motion's image. Perhaps that is why people tend to turn to poetry in emotional and difficult times. Also, there's potentially more freedom to be private and to under-share than in unsent letters or journal entries. Symbolic language and metaphor have a power that allows us to attend to that which is left out, and is perhaps unthinkable (Cixous & Calle-Gruber, 1994/1997). Some of the tools of poetic writing, for example, rhythm (try reading aloud), metaphor and a quality of conciseness are illustrated in the fragments of poetry below:

If she were male
If she were male
She'd be monstrous
Napoleonic Swaggering, bullying
Power loving.
She's a strong red wine
Fine tannins with black cherries
Lively acidity and a
Chocolaty complexion.
Belligerent, beating
The competition
(And even those not competing).
Swearing, smoking, shouting:
"I nearly made him cry"
Agitating, aggressive,
"I don't back down".
And when they asked us
When she retired
To evaluate her management style
We said: "We love her but
She works too hard." (Wright, 2018)

Borrowing from journal entries and from fragments of fiction and poetry that tend to record the negatives, this article might have denied the positives of leaving paid work.

Retired as a purring cat
The days when I stay in bed for a bit.
Grey, cold days when
Scraping ice off the windscreen would have meant an even
Darker, earlier start.
So, with a book, or radio and cup of tea, I lie there.
Retired as a purring cat.

For some, retirement can't come soon enough and is anticipated with joy. Jubilacion.

The fears underlying the decision to move out of that warm water of working life, to let it ebb away, or have the plug pulled abruptly, can be paralysing. Like Maya Angelou, in her poem, 'The last decision', the question arises of what to give up next, but life itself:

> The print is too small, distressing me.
>
> Wavering black things on the page,
>
> Wriggling polliwogs all about.
>
> I know it's my age. I'll have to give up reading. (Angelou, 1986: 96)

Some contemporary poets, such as Hollie McNish or George the Poet perform their words (https://holliepoetry.com/; www.georgethepoet.com/). Imagine you're going to take to the stage one night in a local that hosts 'Guerilla Poetry'. What would you say? Write it down.

## Celebration

Getting away from some of the horrors of working lives is a good reason to retire. Choosing to spend time on cherished hobbies and with family, there may be many causes for celebration in plans for the future without paid work: 'Leaving that job with an early retirement package was the happiest day of my life.'

Given luxuries, like enough money to pay the bills, some retirees luxuriate in the time 'to stand and stare'. In earlier centuries, the leisured classes would have been permanent retirees; now there is a pensioned way out of toil for some working people – they have the space for creativity and the money to pay: daytime classes – singing, Pilates, circle dancing, bowls, foreign holidays, more time with the watercolour painting and other creative hobbies. Their new identity is cause for celebration, away from the toxicities of some workplaces.

Life without paid work, of course, is very different for those without good pensions, who struggle to pay the bills, who need to sort through the reduced vegetables in the supermarket. Others move into more than full-time volunteering. The pressures and pleasures of running the local Oxfam branch or the University of the Third Age (U3A) feel familiar and reassuring. It's like a job without a pay packet. The empty days in the diary are all filled up and there's a feeling of usefulness that is worth a lot in terms of social capital.

Advertisements for the wealthy over-60s feature: cruises, gated retirement communities with swimming pools, Quality Riser Recliners, stair lifts, incontinence pads, machinery and ramps for getting pets in and out of cars. Aimed at a particular and monocultural demographic (a recent article about the writer Alan Bennett in a UK newspaper featured ads for all of the above). I object to the stereotyping. Most advertisements targeted at this group feature images of smiling, whitehaired couples celebrating on a tropical beach hand in hand (the couples are usually heterosexual); or sitting by the log burner, along with the pedigree Labrador (the kennels will pamper him when they finish that expensive wine and decide on another spa-break). After all, privileged and blessed with no mortgage and big pensions, some of my peer group would argue that retirement is their due: one long holiday.

## Dream journals

The landscape of growing old is not pretty – for some. The decline of taken-for-granted health – the physicality of ageing, curved spines, arthritis, hair-loss, toothlessness, high blood pressure and the consequent losses of vanity, mobility and independence – can be full of fear. Asking for help may not be easy and shame seems to be part of the package. Retirement from paid work is the anteroom to death, after all, and if we take a pessimistic view, that's all there is to it: dementia, stroke, chronic illnesses await.

Writing can be less exposing, less shaming in managing those feelings than face-to-face conversations – even, perhaps especially, with counsellors. Shame is connected to loss of identity as part of the workforce and connected to leaving part of a younger stage of life. Shame is felt, as well, with the various physical indicators of declining years: can't hear – poor old thing; can't see – scrabbling about in the bag for the glasses; and worse. We won't approach incontinence – yet. Telling stories to ourselves in writing is a way of reclaiming ourselves before risking saying the words out loud (Etherington, 2003).

Some prefer to draw, to sing, to take photographs as their way of expressing themselves, including the feelings of shame, fear and depression that might accompany retirement. Combining these creative methods with writing is fun, and again, more fun in a group (Rogers, 1993/2000). The risks of boredom and isolation are overcome by replacing paid work with unpaid – yet ... Even volunteering carries a risk of shame:

> Didn't think there'd be an interview. I looked at the job description and thought I could do that. It's an entry-level job – that's how I got into the voluntary sector 40 years ago! Now they are shortlisting and interviewing, and it's all unpaid. Imagine if I didn't get it!

## Resistance and dialogues

Certainly, although not the major focus of this article, retirement is a gendered story. Leslie, the reluctant retiree (RR) chooses to write a dialogue with an optimistic and cheery part of herself about the differences between her and her happily retired partner, Gordon. She calls this upbeat part of her, 'the life begins at 60' or LBA.

The reluctant
retiree (RR):            I'm bored.

The Life Begins
At60 retiree (LBA):   Well, go out then – 10,000 steps a day remember.

| | |
|---|---|
| RR: | It's cold and I'd rather listen to the radio, but I can't work this new digital one. Anyway, it'll be dark by 3 and it's half past 2 now. |
| LBA: | You need a time-table – go on – schedule all those Pilates classes, picking up the grandchildren every other day, canvassing for the Green Party, volunteering at the library, walking the dog, University of the Third Age foreign film group, choir, Latin dancing, oil-painting for beginners ... |
| RR: | I need a job. I'm bored. When I think of that lot, I'm tired and bored. |
| LBA: | Gordon's not bored. He's out early every day, using his bus pass to get down at the boat yard. He meets his mates, has a brew-up – he's never been so happy. "Should have done it years ago," is what he's saying about retiring. He's always asking you to go with him, help with the cleaning, get together with the other wives. |
| RR: | Why do you think I want to go back to work? Sitting around some freezing cold club room on a damp canal towpath, talking about cleaning fluids – no thank you. Work was a much better distraction. |
| LBA: | Don't get grumpy. People don't like grumpy. |

Even the status and potential cushioning of voluntary responsibilities can't prevent the undermining behaviour experienced from younger people. Leslie says of a nurse: 'She is treating me like a little old woman.' Some little old women are happy grandmothers, and some are not. Leslie writes:

> Sitting in parks in the drizzle, scraping dog-shit off kids' shoes, boring afternoons when the grandchildren have gone and nobody to talk to except Gordon ... this is no life.

The privacy of writing is key. Gordon won't read this writing. Leslie writes online, password protected, and sometimes even deletes what she's written. Leslie uses writing to resist being poured into the moulds waiting for her to settle into now she's no longer 'out at work'.

Jane Speedy's very alive, illustrated book about life after a stroke in her late fifties is made up of layers of fragmented poetic text and full-colour images (Speedy, 2015). It is not a stroke memoir, neither is its major focus the leaving of a professional career although changes in working life and identity are central. It's about resistance: 'This is my embodied/visceral/textual resistance to narrative coherence and my means of bringing experience to life ... I am giving an account of this life as an act of homage or gratitude. I am so glad that I am not dead' (Speedy, 2015: 14).

'Grounded' from her work as an academic, Speedy writes about the fear of certain nurses, shared by the 'confused elderly women' she was in hospital with. 'Having known these women, however, I now no longer fear old age' (Speedy, 2015: 15).

---

## Activity 10.2

Write to a part of your body you're worried about. Start with Dear ... back, knee or whatever you choose. Then, write the reply from your back, knee ...

---

One way to resist has always been to join with others. The creation of writing groups for those who are thinking of retiring or have finally left the paid job is a rich alternative to one-to-one counselling. Such groups, whether facilitated by therapists, creative writers, neither or both are illustrated by some of the writing by members of Lapidus, an international 'Words for Wellbeing' association. Lapidus publishes a journal, holds conferences and advertises groups and workshops mostly in the UK (www.lapidus.org.uk) and increasingly elsewhere around the world.

Encouraging written expression is very much part of my practice, at the moment mostly in writing groups rather than with individuals (Wright, 2012). There is solidarity in groups.

## Writing groups

> The process felt both powerful and liberating. Being able to answer as my 'other person' in the dialogue activity was surprising; in fact, the answer was not what I expected at all, even though I wrote it myself. (Feedback from a UK self-writing group participant)

The setting: the room, a corporate and rather too carpeted space, is changed when the coloured paper, pens, pencils, pastels, and music arrive.

We are due to spend three hours together and have some materials, online and in paper form, as support. Posters around the room say: 'Gag the inner critic!', 'Spelling and grammar don't matter', 'Forget school rules.' It is made clear in the 'ground-rules' that we are here not to produce works of art, poems or prose to be judged and evaluated. This writing is different and is 'for your eyes only until and if you choose to share it'.

Tony is one of 16 people in the group. He has been asked to think about a recent experience when he felt a strong emotion, noticing how feelings work in the body. Tony's struggle with writing seems to be freed up:

> If I can't say what's been happening out loud to another human being and I can't write it down what can I do? What do I like doing, they ask? Dancing. Lately I haven't been dancing much, but the wedding at the weekend was great. One of the bands

was a combination of Irish jigs and reels plus – I couldn't stop myself dancing. It's a tonic to move around to music in a group of other people. I stood watching for a while, too hot to carry on. What happened to the playful me?

Tony uses a written dialogue with different parts of himself, as in Matt Haig's writing through depression which a friend has loaned him (Haig, 2015):

DANCER: you don't do this often enough. The music has a real impact on you, right through your feet to the top of your head – and the dancing even more so. What stops you dancing more?

WORK ETHIC: it's all right for you. You haven't got bills at the back of your mind all the time, and people pressurising you.

DANCER: all work and no play .... anyway, you're going to leave all that behind in another month. Retirement – yay!

ANXIOUS: I was worried all the way there thinking you wouldn't be able to find your way there to that wedding. And then you had to drive back and I knew you'd get lost.

FROZEN ONE: Silence.

DANCER: You did get there and you got home okay. And you felt better ...

ANXIOUS: Yes, I did – for a while. I was worried you'd feel tired all day after all that dancing though, and you did.

Memoir writing, creative writing classes, retirement and transition writing groups are all part of the same process. They involve writing (and reading) words that are close to life. The Irish writer, Nuala O'Faolin writes in her memoir:

> There is an idea current in the prevailing culture that writing about something that pains you heals the pain. I was not, when I began writing my life story, and am not now, healed of my mother. But you do gain a small distance from anything by keeping it in suspension in your mind while you work at finding the words to fit it. The process is so slow and incremental that you don't notice its effect, but the point is that it is a process ... (O'Faolain, 2003: 36)

Yes, it is a process of, and perhaps it can only be understood by trying it out.

## Endings

Not all choose to retire, to end their paid work, or find the decision easy, even if the choice is theirs. Tools from creative writing, and especially writing in groups, eases the isolation and allows emotional expression. Feedback from writing groups includes, 'It's like reading my own mind', and, 'It seems to be all in body, mind, spirit'.

This chapter has focused on a transition; the metaphor about the warm bathwater of working life slowly ebbing away might capture the experience for some. Others might resonate more with a feeling of the bath plug being yanked and a cold shower turned on. The grey pound may well be powerful, but life without work is a challenge – even more so if there aren't enough pounds in the pension to cover the cost of living. For others, retirement means enjoying all that work got in the way of, hobbies, family, holidays and all – none the less, this shift represents a transition which can be challenging.

A dilemma with autoethnographic and writing as inquiry intended for publication is how to manage the ethical tensions, but for those who use therapeutic writing for their own private purposes, publication is not the point. Writing creatively, and particularly in groups, can be a way to connect with self, others and sometimes a wider audience during times of transition. This kind of writing is about imagination and intuition, with rational thinking and intellect taking a back seat, as with most forms of creativity. The tools of creative writing are simple, need no special equipment – and can be adapted for self-help, group work and for any kind of reflection.

## Acknowledgement

An earlier version of this chapter was published in 2018 as: The warm bathwater of working life slowly ebbing away, *British Journal of Guidance and Counselling*, *46*(3), 293–309. It can be accessed at www.tandfonline.com/eprint/BbJIvpja 9jF6thTbdj9k/full. Reprinted with permission of Taylor and Francis Ltd.

# References

Adams, M. (2014). *The myth of the untroubled therapist. Private life, professional practice.* London: Routledge.

Adams, T. E., Holman Jones, S., & Ellis, C. (2015). *Autoethnography: Understanding qualitative research.* New York: Oxford University Press.

Aguinaldo, J. P. (2004). Rethinking validity in qualitative research from a social constructionist perspective: From 'Is this valid research?' to 'What is this research valid for?'. *The Qualitative Report, 1*(3), 127–136.

Allport, G. W. (1962). The general and the unique in psychological science. *Journal of Personality, 30*, 405–422.

Alvesson, M., & Skoldeberg, K. (2000). *Reflexive methodology.* London: SAGE.

American Psychological Association. (2013). Recognition of psychotherapy effectiveness. *Journal of Psychotherapy Integration, 23*(3), 320–330.

Anderson, A., Knowles, Z., & Gilbourne, D. (2004). Reflective practice for sport psychologists: Concepts, models, practical implications, and thoughts on dissemination. *The Sport Psychologist, 18*, 188–203.

Anderson, R., & Braud, W. (2011). *Transforming self and others through research.* Albany, New York: Suny Press.

Angelou, M. (1986). *And still I rise.* London: Virago Press.

Argyris, C., & Schön, D. (1978). *Organizational learning: A theory of action perspective.* Reading, MA: Addison Wesley.

Argyris, C., Putnam, R., & Smith, D. (1985). *Action science: Concepts, methods and skills for research intervention.* San Francisco, CA: Jossey-Bass.

Auger, R. (2013). Autism spectrum disorders: A research review for school counselors. *Professional School Counseling, 16*(4), 256–268.

Aujoulat, I., Luminet, O., & Deccache, A. (2007). The perspective of patients on their experience of powerlessness. *Qualitative Health Research, 17*(6), 772–785.

Aveyard, H., and Sharp, P. (2009). *A beginner's guide to evidence based practice in health and social care.* Maidenhead: Open University Press.

BACP. (2018). Ethical framework for good practice in counselling and psychotherapy. Lutterworth: BACP. Retrieved from www.bacp.co.uk/media/3103/bacp-ethical-framework-for-the-counselling-professions-2018.pdf.

Bademcia, O., Warfab, N., Bagdatlı-Vuralc, E., Karadayid, S., & Karasarf, S. (2019). Teachers' perceptions of an attachment-informed psychosocial programme for schoolchildren with social and emotional problems in Istanbul, Turkey. *Journal of Social Work Practice*, 1–3. Doi: 10.1080/02650533.2019.1611550

Bager-Charleson, S. (2010). *Why do therapists choose to be therapists?* London: Karnac Books.

Bager-Charleson, S., & Kasap, Z. (2017). Embodied situatedness and emotional entanglement in research – An autoethnographic hybrid inquiry into the experience of doing data analysis. *Counselling and Psychotherapy Research, 17*(3), 190–200.

Bager-Charleson, S., Dewaele, J-M., Costa, B., & Kasap, Z. (2017). A multilingual outlook: Can awareness-raising about multilingualism affect therapists' practice? A mixed-method evaluation. *Language and Psychoanalysis, 6*(2), 1–21.

Bager-Charleson, S., Du Plock, S., & McBeath, A. (2018). Therapists have a lot to add to the field of research, but many don't make it there: A narrative thematic inquiry into counsellors' and psychotherapists' embodied engagement with research. *Language and Psychoanalysis, 7*(1), 4–22.

Bager-Charleson, S., & van Rijn, B. (2011). *Assessment in counselling and psychotherapy.* Exeter: Learning Matters.

Baldwin, S. A., & Imel, Z. E. (2013). Therapist effects: Findings and methods. In M. J. Lambert (Ed.), *Handbook of psychotherapy and behavior change* (6th ed., pp. 258–297). Hoboken, NJ: John Wiley.

Bamberg, M. (1997). Positioning between structure and performance. *Journal of Narrative and Life History, 7*(1–4), 335–342.

Barber, P. (2006). *Becoming a practitioner researcher: A gestalt approach to holistic inquiry.* London: Middlesex University.

Barkham, M., Hardy, G. E., & Mellor-Clark, J. (Eds.). (2010). *Developing and delivering practice-based evidence: A guide for the psychological therapies.* London: John Wiley & Sons.

Barkham, M., Mellor-Clark, J., & Stiles, W. B. (2015). A CORE approach to progress monitoring and feedback: Enhancing evidence and improving practice. *Psychotherapy, 52*(4), 402–411.

Barton, J. (2019). *Progressive (dis)ability: The experience of living with Charcot-Marie-Tooth disease.* Doctoral Dissertation. Middlesex University and Metanoia Institute Doctor of Counselling Psychology and Psychotherapy by Professional Studies.

Behar, R. (1996). *The vulnerable observer: Anthropology that breaks your heart.* Boston, MA: Beacon Press.

Berne, E. (1964). *Games people play.* New York: Grove Press.

Beutler, L. E., Williams, R. E., Wakefield, P. J., & Entwistle, S. R. (1995). Bridging scientist and practitioner perspectives in clinical psychology. *American Psychologist, 50,* 984–994. http://dx.doi.org/10.1037/0003-066X.50.12.984

Bick, E. (1964). Notes on infant observation in psychoanalytic training. *International Journal of Psychoanalysis, 49,* 484–486.

Binks, C., Jones, F., & Knight, K. (2013). Facilitating reflective practice groups in clinical psychology training: A phenomenological study. *Reflective Practice, 14*(3), 1–14.

Black, P. E., & Plowright, D. (2010). A multi-dimensional model of reflective learning for professional development. *Reflective Practice, 11*(2), 245–258.

Boden, Z., Gibson, S., Owen, G. J., & Benson, O. (2016). Feelings and intersubjectivity in qualitative suicide research. *Qualitative Health Research, 26,* 1078–1090.

Bohart, A. C., & Greaves Wade, A. (2013). The client in psychotherapy. In M. J. Lambert (Ed.), *Handbook of psychotherapy and behaviour change* (6th ed., pp. 219–257). Hoboken, NJ: John Wiley & Sons.

Boisvert, C., & Faust, D. (2006). Practicing psychologists' knowledge of general psychotherapy research findings: Implications for science practice relations. *Professional Psychology: Research and Practice, 37,* 708–716.

Bolton, G. (2005/2018). *Reflective practice – Writing and professional development.* London: SAGE.

Bolton, G. (2011). *Write yourself: Creative writing and personal development.* London: Jessica Kingsley.

Bolton, G., Field, V., & Thomson, K. (2006). *Writing works. A resource handbook.* London: Jessica Kingsley.

Bondi, L. (2013). Research and therapy generating meaning and feeling gaps. *Qualitative Inquiry, 19,* 9–19.

Bondi, L., & Fewell, J. (2016). *Practitioner research in counselling and psychotherapy. The power of examples.* London: Palgrave Macmillan.

Bordin, E. S. (1979). The generalizability of the psychoanalytic concept of the working alliance. *Psychotherapy: Theory, Research, Practice, 16*(3), 252–260.

Bowlby, J. (1969). *Attachment and Loss, Vol. 1: Attachment*. New York: Basic Books.

Brande, D. (1934/1996). *Becoming a writer*. London: Macmillan.

Braun, V., & Clarke, V. (2006). Using thematic analysis in psychology. *Qualitative Research in Psychology, 3*, 77–101.

Buber, M. (1947/1971). *Between man & man*. Glasgow: Fontana Library.

Bryman, A. (2001). *Social research methods*. Oxford: Oxford University Press.

Bury, M. (1991). The sociology of chronic illness: A review of research and prospects. *Sociology of Health and Illness, 13*(4), 451–468.

Carroll, M., & Gilbert, M. (2005). *On being a supervisee*. London: Vulkani Publishing.

Carter, D., & Gradin, S. (2001). *Writing as reflective action: A reader*. New York: LongmanPearson.

Chang, L. C., Li, I. C., & Liu, C. H. (2004). A study of the empowerment process for cancer patients using Freire's dialogical interviewing. *Journal of Nursing Research, 12*(1), 41–49.

Charmaz, K. (1983). Loss of self: A fundamental form of suffering in the chronically ill. *Sociology of Health and Illness, 5*(2), 168–195.

Charon, R. (2006). *Narrative medicine: Honouring the stories of illness*. New York: Oxford University Press.

Chase, S. E. (2005). Narrative inquiry: Multiple lenses, approaches and voices. In N. K. Denzin & Y. S. Lincoln (Eds.), *The Sage handbook of qualitative research* (3rd ed., pp. 651–679). Thousand Oaks, CA: SAGE.

Cixous, H., & Calle-Gruber, M. (1994/1997). *Rootprints: Memory and life writing*. London: Routledge.

Clark, J. N., & James, S. (2003). The radicalized self: The impact on the self of the contested nature of the diagnosis of chronic fatigue syndrome. *Social Science and Medicine, 57*(8), 1387–1395.

Clarke, S., & Hoggett, P. (Eds.) (2009). *Researching beneath the surface: Psychosocial research methods in practice*. London: Taylor & Francis.

Clarkson, P. (2002). *The therapeutic relationship*. London: Whurr.

Connell, J., Barkham, M., & Mellor-Clark, J. (2008). The effectiveness of UK student counselling services: An analysis using the CORE System. *British Journal of Guidance & Counselling, 36*(1), 1–18.

Cooper, M. (2008). *Essential research findings in counselling and psychotherapy: The facts are friendly*. London: SAGE.

Cooper, M. (2013). Experiencing relational depth in therapy: What we know so far. In D. Knox, S. Murphy, & M. Wiggins Cooper (Eds.), *Relational depth: New perspectives and developments* (pp. 62–76). Basingstoke: Palgrave.

Cooper, M., & McLeod, J. (2011). *Pluralistic counselling and psychotherapy*. London: SAGE.

Cooper, M., & Norcross, J. C. (2016). A brief, multidimensional measure of clients' therapy preferences: The Cooper-Norcross Inventory of Preferences (C-NIP). *International Journal of Clinical and Health Psychology, 16*(1), 87–98.

Corbin, J., & Strauss, A. (1987). Accompaniments of chronic illness: Changes in body, self, biography, and biological time. *Research in the Sociology of Health Care, 6*, 249–281.

CORE Information Management Systems Ltd. (2007). CORE Net. Retrieved from www.coreims-online.co.uk.

Cozolino, L. (2002). *The neuroscience of human relationships: Attachment and the developing social brain*. New York: Norton Press.

Creswell, J., & Clark, V. L. (2011). *Designing and conducting mixed methods research*. London: SAGE.

CSIP. (2008). *Improving access to psychological therapies (IAPT) Commissioning Toolkit*. Department of Health. https://www.uea.ac.uk/documents/246046/11991919/ IAPT + Commissioning + Toolkit + 2008 + .pdf/cc6a4f24-dc6b-45d9-a631-ffdd075c6f0a

Cuijpers, P., van Straten, A., & Andersson, G. (2008). Internet-administered cognitive behavior therapy for health problems: A systematic review. *Journal of behavioural medicine, 31*(2), 169–177.

Datler, W., Laxar, R., & Trunkenpolz, K. (2012) Observation in nursing home. In C. Urwin and J. Sternberg (Eds.), *Infant observation and research: Emotional processes in everyday lives* (pp. 160–171). Hove and New York: Routledge.

Deary, V. (2007). CFS and the facts of life – an article for clinicians. Available at: https://www.kcl.ac.uk/ioppn/depts/pm/research/cfs/health/index (accessed 28 January 2020).

Denzin, N. K. (2009). *On understanding emotion*. New Brunswick, NJ: Transaction Publishers. (Original work published 1984).

Descartes, R. (1941/2008). Mediations on first philosophy. In J. Cottingham (Ed.), *Western philosophy* (2nd ed., pp. 22–25). Oxford: Blackwell.

Devon, A. (2017). CBT versus the unconscious. Ignore countertransference at your peril. In P. Valerio, *Introduction to countertransference in therapy* (pp. 81–97). London: Routledge.

Douglas, K., & Carless, D. (2016). Qualitative conversations: Tony E. Adams [Video file]. Retrieved from www.youtube.com/watch?v = 7nTX3BkUrmA (Accessed 20 September 2018).

du Plock, S. (Ed.). (2004). What do we mean when we use the word 'research'? *Existential Analysis, 15*(1), 29–37.

Eleftheriadou, Z. (2010). *Psychotherapy and culture*. London: Karnac Books.

Elliott, R. (1993). Helpful Aspects of Therapy Form. Retrieved from www.experiential-researchers.org/instruments/elliott/hat.pdf.

Elliott, R., Bohart, A. C., Watson, J. C., & Murphy, D. (2018). Therapist empathy and client outcome: An updated meta-analysis. *Psychotherapy, 55*(4), 399–410.

Elliott, R., Watson, J., Greenberg, L. S., Timulak, L., & Freire, E. (2013). Research on humanistic-experiential psychotherapies. In M. J. Lambert (Ed.), *Bergin & Garfield's handbook of psychotherapy and behaviour change* (6th ed., pp. 495–538). New York: Wiley.

Ellis, D., & Tucker, I. (2015). *Social psychology of emotions*. London: SAGE.

Etherington, K. (2004). *Becoming a reflexive researcher: Using our selves in research*. London: Jessica Kingsley.

Etherington, K. (2003). *Trauma, the body and transformation*. London: Jessica Kingsley.

Finlay, L., & Gough, B. (2003). *Reflexivity: A practical guide for researchers in health and social science*. London: Blackwell.

Finlay, L. (2016). Being a therapist-researcher: Doing relational-reflexive research. *UKCP: The Psychotherapist, 62*, 4–5.

Folkes-Skinner, J., Elliott, R., & Wheeler, S. (2010). 'A baptism of fire': A qualitative investigation of trainee counsellors' experience at the start of training. *Counselling and Psychotherapy Research, 10*(2), 83–92.

Fonagy, P., Gergeley, G., Jurist, E. J., & Target, M. I. (2002). *Affect regulation, mentalization, and the development of the self*. New York: Other Press.

Fook, J. (2002). *Social work: Critical theory and practice*. London: SAGE.

Fook, J. (2008). Critical reflection: A review of contemporary literature and understandings. In S. White, J. Fook, & F. Gardner (Eds.), *Critical reflection in health and social care* (pp. 3–20). Maidenhead: Open University Press.

Foucault, M. (1984). Madness and civilisation: The birth of the asylum. In P. Rabinow (Ed.), *The Foucault reader: An introduction to Foucault's thoughts* (pp. 141–168). London: Penguin Books.

Frawley-O'Dea, M., & Sarnat, J. (2001). *The supervisory relationship*. New York and London: Guilford Press.

Freud, S. (1938/1959). *An outline of psycho-analysis*. London: The Hogarth Press.

Freudenberger, S. (2004). Interculturalism, transculturalism and the problem of 'meaning'. In H. Sandkuhler & H.-B. Lim (Eds.), *Transculturality: Epistemology, ethics and politics* (pp. 39–50). Berlin, Germany: Peter Lang.

Friedman, V. J. (2001). Action science: Creating communities of inquiry in communities of practice. In P. Reason & H. Bradbury (Eds.), *Handbook of action research: Participative inquiry and practice* (pp. 150–170). London: SAGE.

Gendlin, E. (1997). *A process model*. New York: The Focusing Institute.

Gendlin, E. T. (2009). What first and third person processes really are. *Journal of Consciousness Studies, 16*(10–12), 332–362.

Ghaemi, S. N. (2007). *The concepts of psychiatry: A pluralistic approach to the mind and mental illness*. Baltimore, MD: Johns Hopkins University Press.

Gibbs, G. (1988). *Learning by doing: A guide to teaching and learning methods*. Oxford: Oxford Brookes University Further Education Unit.

Gibbs, G. (2013). Reflections on the changing nature of educational development. *International Journal for Academic Development, 18*(1), 4–14.

Goulet, M. H., Larue, C., & Alderson, M. (2016). Reflective practice: A comparative dimensional analysis of the concept in nursing and education studies. *Nursing forum, 51*(2), 139–150.

Grant, M., & Booth, A. (2009). A typology of reviews: an analysis of 14 review types and associated methodologies. *Health Information and Library Journal, 26*(2), 91–108.

Greenberg, M., Shergill, S. S., Szmukler, G., & Tantam, D. (2003). *Narrative in psyhiatry*. London: Jessica Kingsley.

Guggenbuhl-Craig, A. (1991). Quacks, charlatans and false prophets. In C. Sweig & J. Abrams (Eds.), *Meeting the shadow* (pp. 110–116). New York: Penguin.

Habermas, J. (1987). *The theory of communicative action* (Vol. 2). Boston, MA: Beacon Press.

Haig, M. (2015). *Reasons to stay alive*. Edinburgh: Canongate Books.

Haraway, D. (1988). Situated knowledges: The science question in feminism and the privilege of partial perspective. *Feminist Studies, 14*(3), 575–599.

Hargaden, H., & Sills, C. (2002). *Transactional analysis: A relational perspective*. New York: Brunner-Routledge.

Hawkins, P., & Shohet, R. (2005). *Supervision in the helping professions*. Maidenhead: Open University Press.

Heron, J., & Reason, P. (2001). The practice of co-operative inquiry. In P. Reason & H. Bradbury (Eds.), *Handbook of action research: Participative inquiry and practice* (pp. 179–188). London: SAGE.

Holloway, W., & Jefferson, T. (2000). *Doing qualitative research differently: Free association, narrative and the interview method*. London and New Delhi: Sage.

Hollway, W. (2009). Applying the 'experience-near' principle to research: Psychoanalytically informed methods. *Journal of Social Work Practice, 23*, 461–474.

Hollway, W. (2011). In between external and internal worlds: Imagination in Transitional Space. *UK Methodological Innovations Online, 6*, 50–60. Retrieved from http://www.pbs.plym.ac.uk/mi/pdf/8-02-12/MIO63Paper23.pdf

Holman Jones, S., Adams, T. E., & Ellis, C. (Eds.). (2013). *Handbook of autoethnography*. Walnut Creek, CA: Left Coast Press.

Holmes, J., & Lindley, R. (1998). *The values of psychotherapy*. London: Karnac Books.

Horvath, A. O., Del Re, A. C., Fluckiger, C., & Symonds, D. (2011). Alliance in Individual Psychotherapy. In J. C. Norcross (Ed.), *Psychotherapy relationships that work: Evidence-based responsiveness* (2nd ed., pp. 25–69). Oxford: Oxford University Press.

Hoshmand, L. T., & Polkinghorne, D. E. (1992). Redefining the science–practice relationship and professional training, education and training. *Psychology, 47*(1), 55–66.

Huang, T., Hill, C., & Gelso, C. (2013). Psychotherapy engagers versus non-engagers: Differences in alliance, therapist verbal response modes, and client attachment. *Psychotherapy Research, 23*(5), 568–577.

Hunt, C. (2000). *Therapeutic dimensions of autobiography in creative writing*. London: Jessica Kingsley.

Hunt, C., & Sampson, F. (Eds.). (2002). *The self on the page: Theory and practice of creative writing in personal development*. London: Jessica Kingsley.

Inskipp, F., & Proctor, B. (2001). *Making the most of supervision* (Part 1). Twickenham: Cascade.

Ixer, G. (2016). The concept of reflection: Is it skill based or values? *Social Work Education, 35*(7), 809–824.

Jay, J. K., & Johnson, K. L. (2002). Capturing complexity: A typology of reflective practice for teacher education. *Teaching and Teacher Education, 18*(1), 73–85.

Johns, C. (1995). Framing learning through reflection within Carper's fundamental ways of knowing in nursing. *Journal of Advanced Nursing, 22*, 226–234.

Jones, R. L., & Wallace, M. (2005). Another bad day at the training ground: Coping with ambiguity in the coaching context. *Sport, Education and Society, 10*(1), 119–134.

Josselson, R. (2011). 'Bet you think this song is about you': Whose narrative is it in narrative research? *Fielding Graduate University*: Available at Journals.hil.unb.ca/index.php/NW/article/download/18472/19971

Josselson, R. (2013). *Interviewing for qualitative inquiry. A relational approach*. New York: Guilford Press.

Kagan, N. (1967). *Studies in human interaction: Interpersonal process recall stimulated by videotape*. East Lansing, MI: East Lansing College of Education, Michigan State University.

Kant, I. (1781/2007). *Critique of Pure Reason* (Trans. M. Weigelt). London: Penguin.

Klann Thullesen. M. (2019). Psychological work with survivors of sex trafficking: A narrative inquiry of the impact on practitioners (Doctoral dissertation). London: Metanoia Institute.

Klein, R., Bernard, H. S., & Shermer, V. (Eds.) (2011). *On becoming a psychotherapist: The personal and professional journey*. Oxford and New York: Oxford University Press.

Knox, R. (2008) Clients' experiences of relational depth in person-centred counselling. *Counselling and Psychotherapy Research, 8*(3), 182–188.

Knox, R., Murphy, D., Wiggins, S., & Cooper, M. (Eds.). *Relational depth: New perspectives and developments*. Basingstoke: Palgrave.

Kolb, D. A. (2014). *Experiential learning: Experience as the source of learning and development*. New Jersey: Pearson Education Ltd.

Kolb, D. A. (1984). *Experiential Learning: Experience as the Source of learning and development*. New Jersey: Prentice-Hall.

Kottler, J. (2011). *On being a therapist* (4th revised ed.). San Francisco: Jossey Bass.

Kroenke, K., Spitzer, R. L., & Williams, J. B. (2001). The PHQ-9: Validity of a brief depression severity measure. *Journal of General and Internal Medicine, 16*, 606–613.

Ladany, N., Mori, Y., & Mehr, K. (2012). Effective and ineffective supervision. *The Counseling Psychologist, 41*(1): 28–47. https://doi.org/10.1177/0011000012442648

Lambert, M. J., & Barley, E. D. (2002). Research summary on the therapeutic relationship and psychotherapy outcome. In J. C. Norcross (Ed.), *Psychotherapy relationships that work: Therapist contributions and responsiveness to patients* (pp. 17–32). Oxford: Oxford University Press.

Lambert, M. J., & Shimokawa, K. (2011). Collecting client feedback. In J. Norcross, & M. J. Lambert (Eds.), *Psychotherapy relationships that work*. (2nd ed., pp. 203–223). Oxford: Oxford University Press.

Lambert, M. J., Whipple, J. L., & Kleinstäuber, M. (2018). Collecting and delivering progress feedback: A meta-analysis of routine outcome monitoring. *Psychotherapy, 55*(4), 520–537.

Lambert, M. J., Whipple, J. L., Vermeersch, D. A. D., Smart, W., Hawkins, E. J., Nielsen, S. L., & Goates, M. (2002). Enhancing psychotherapy outcomes via providing feedback on client progress: A replication. *Clinical Psychology & Psychotherapy, 9*(2), 91–103.

Lapworth, P., & Sills, C. (2011). *Integration in counselling and psychotherapy*. London: SAGE.

Lengelle, R., & Meijers, F. (2014). Narrative identity: Writing the self in career learning. *British Journal of Guidance and Counselling, 42*(1), 52–72.

Lewis, D., Virden. T., Hutchings, P., Smith, E., & Bhargava, R. (2011). Competence assessment integrating reflective practice in a professional psychology program. *Journal of the Scholarship of Teaching and Learning, 11*(3), 86–106.

MacMahon, P. (2019). Integrative therapists' clinical experiences of personal blind spots. An interpretative phenomenological analysis. (Doctoral dissertation). London: Metanoia Institute.

Marshall, T. (2019). The concept of reflection: A systematic review and thematic synthesis across professional contexts, *Reflective Practice, 20*(3), 396–415.

May, R., Angel, E., & Ellenberger, H. F. (Eds.). (1979). *Existence: A new dimension in psychiatry and psychology*. New York: Basic Books.

McBeath, A. (2019). The Motivations of psychotherapists: An in-depth survey. *Counselling and Psychotherapy Research, 19*, 377–387.

McLeod, J. (1994). *Doing counselling research*. London: SAGE.

McLeod, J. (2007). *Counselling skills*. Maidenhead: Open University Press.

McLeod, J., & Balamoutsou, S. (2001). A method for qualitative narrative analysis of psychotherapy transcripts. In *Qualitative psychotherapy research* (pp. 121–153). Berlin: Psychologische Beitrage.

McWilliam, C. L., Stewart, M., Brown, J. B., McNair, S., Desai, K., & Patterson, M. L. (1996). Creating empowering meaning: An interactive process of promoting health with chronically ill older Canadians. *Health Promotion International, 12*(2), 111–123.

Mearns, D., & Cooper, M. (2005/2018). *Working at relational depth in counselling and psychotherapy*. London: SAGE.

Merleau-Ponty, M. (1999). The phenomenology of perception. In M. Friedman (Ed.), *The worlds of existentialism: A critical reader*. New York: Humanities Books.

Messer, S. (2004). Evidence-based practice: beyond empirically supported treatments. *American Psychological Association. Professional Psychology: Research and Practice, 35*(6), 580–588.

Mezirow, J. (2009). Transformative learning theory. In J. Mezirow & E. W. Taylor (Eds.), *Transformative learning in practice: Insights from community, workplace and higher education* (pp. 18–32). New York: Jossey Bass.

Miller, A. (1997). *The drama of the gifted child: The search for the true self*. New York: Basic Books.

Miller, S. D., Duncan, B. L., & Johnson, L. (2002). Session Rating Scale (SRS.V.3.0). Retrieved from www.talkingcure.com.

Morrow-Bradley, C., & Elliott, R. (1986). Utilization of psychotherapy research by practicing psychotherapists. *American Psychologist,* Special Issue: Psychotherapy Research, *41,* 188–197.

Moule, P., & Hek, G. (2011). *Making sense of research.* London: SAGE.

Muran, J. C., Safran, J. D., & Eubanks-Carter, C. (2010). Developing therapist abilities to negotiate alliance ruptures. In J. C. Muran & J. P. Barber (Eds.), *The therapeutic alliance: An evidence-based guide to practice* (pp. 320–340). New York: Guilford Press.

National Institute for Health and Care Excellence. (forthcoming). *Depression in Adults: treatment and management.* Retrieved from www.nice.org.uk/guidance/indevelop ment/gid-cgwave0725/documents.

National Institute for Health and Clinical Excellence. (2009). *Depression treatment and management of depression in adults, including adults with a chronic physical health problem.* Retrieved from www.nice.org.uk/nicemedia/live/12329/45890/45890.pdf.

National Institute for Health and Clinical Excellence. (2004, December, with amendments in April 2007). *Anxiety: Management of anxiety in adults in primary, secondary and community care.* Retrieved from www.nice.org.uk/nicemedia/pdf/CG022quick refguideamended.pdf.

Neuhaus, E. S. (2011). Becoming a cognitive-behavioural therapist. In R. Klein, H. S. Bernard, & V. Shermer (Eds.), *On becoming a psychotherapist: The personal and professional journey* (pp. 212–244). Oxford and New York: Oxford University Press.

Nguyen, Q. D., Fernandez, N., Karsenti, T., & Charlin, B. (2014). What is reflection? A conceptual analysis of major definitions and a proposal of a five-component model. *Medical Education, 48*(12), 1176–1189.

Norcross, J. C. (1990). An eclectic definition of psychotherapy. In J. K. Zeig & W. M. Munion (Eds.), *What is psychotherapy? Contemporary perspectives* (pp. 218–220). San Francisco, CA: Jossey-Bass.

Norcross, J. C. (2002). *Psychotherapy relationships that work: Therapist contributions and responsiveness to patients.* New York: Oxford University Press.

Norcross, J. C. (2011). *Psychotherapy relationships that work: Evidence-based responsiveness* (2nd ed.). New York: Oxford University Press.

Norcross, J. C., & Lambert, M. J. (2018). Psychotherapy relationships that work III. *Psychotherapy, 55*(4), 303–315.

Norcross, J. C., & Prochaska, J. (1983). Psychotherapists in independent practice: Some findings and issues. *Professional Psychology: Research and Practice, 14,* 869–881.

O'Faolain, N. (2003). *Almost there: The onward journey of a Dublin woman, a memoir.* New York: Riverhead Books.

Olkin, R. (1999). *What psychotherapists should know about disability.* New York: The Guilford Press.

Orange, D. M. (1996). *Emotional understanding: Studies in psychoanalytic epistemology.* New York: Guilford Press.

Orange, D. M. (2009). *Thinking for clinicians: Philosophical resources for contemporary psychoanalysis and the humanistic psychotherapies.* Abington: Routledge.

Orlinsky, D., & Ronnestad, M. H. (2005). *How psychotherapists develop: A study of therapeutic work and professional growth.* Washington, DC: APA.

Page, S. (1999). *The shadow and the counsellor.* London: Routledge.

Page, S., & Wosket, V. (2006). *Supervising the counsellor: A cyclical model* (2nd ed.). London and New York: Routledge.

Park, P. (2001). Knowledge and participatory research. In P. Reason & H. Bradbury (Eds.), *Handbook of action research: Participative inquiry and practice* (pp. 81–90). London: SAGE.

Paterson, B. (2001). Myth of empowerment in chronic illness. *Journal of Advanced Nursing, 34*(5), 574–581.

Pelias, R. J. (2015). The end of an academic career: The desperate attempt to hang on and let go. *Qualitative Inquiry, 8,* 120–127.

Pennebaker, J. W. (1993). Putting stress into words: Health, linguistic and therapeutic implications. *Behaviour Research and Therapy, 31:* 539–548.

Philips, D., Penman, D., & Linnington, L. (1999). *Writing well: Creative writing and mental health.* London: Jessica Kingsley.

Polkinghorne, D. E. (1988). *Narrative knowing and human science.* Albany, NY: State University of New York Press.

Price, H., & Cooper, A. (2012). In the field: Psychoanalytic observation and epistemological realism. In C. Urwin & J. Sternberg (Eds.), *Infant observation and research: Emotional processes in everyday lives* (pp. 55–67). Hove and New York: Routledge.

Racker, H. (2001). *Transference and counter transference.* London: Karnac.

Rennie, D. L., & Fergus, K. D. (2006). Embodied categorizing in the grounded theory method. *Theory and Psychology, 16*(4), 483–503.

Richardson, L., & St. Pierre, E. A. (2005). Writing: A method of inquiry. In N. K. Denzin & Y. S. Lincoln (Eds.), *Handbook of qualitative research* (pp. 959–978). Thousand Oaks, CA: SAGE.

Ritchie, J., Lewis, J., McNaughton Nicholls, C., & Ormston, R. (Eds.) (2014). *Qualitative Research Practice* (2nd ed.). London: Sage.

Rogers, C. (1961). *A therapist's view of psychotherapy.* London: Constable & Co.

Rogers, C. (1995). *A way of being.* New York: Houghton Mifflin.

Rogers, N. (1993/2000). *The creative connection – expressive arts as healing.* Palo Alto: Science and Behaviour Books/PCCS Books.

Rogers, R. R. (2001). Reflection in higher education: A concept analysis. *Innovative Higher Education, 26*(1), 37–57.

Ronnestad, M. H., Orlinsky, D. E., Schröder, T. A., Skovholt, T. M., & Willutzki, U. (2019). The professional development of counsellors and psychotherapists: Implications of empirical studies for supervision, training and practice. *Counselling Psychotherapy Resarch, 19,* 214–230.

Rothschild, B. (2000). *The body remembers. The psychophysiology of trauma and trauma treatment.* New York & London: Norton Press.

Roubal, J., Francesetti, G., & Gecele, M. (2017). Aesthetic diagnosis in Gestalt therapy. *Behavioural Science* (Basel), *7*(4), 70.

Rowan, J., & Jacobs, M. (2003). *The therapist's use of self.* Maidenhead: Open University Press.

Ruth-Sahd, L. (2003). Reflective practice: A critical analysis of data-based studies and implications for nursing education. *Journal of Nursing Education, 42*(11), 488–497.

Safran, J. D., Muran, J. C., & Eubanks-Carter, C. (2011). Repairing alliance ruptures. In J. Norcross & M. Lambert (Eds.), *Psychotherapy relationships that work* (2nd ed., pp. 224–238). Oxford: Oxford University Press.

Safran, J., Abreu, I., Ogilvie, A., & DeMaria, A. (2011). Does psychotherapy research influence the clinical practice of researcher-clinicians? *Clinical Psychology Science and Practice, 18*(4), 357–371.

Saldaña, J. (2009). *The coding manual for qualitative researchers.* London: Sage.

Schön, D., & Rein, M. (1994). *Frame reflection: Toward the resolution of intractable policy controversies.* New York: Basic Books.

Schön, D. A. (1983). *The reflective practitioner: How professionals think in action*. New York: Basic Books.

Sedgwick, D. (2005). *The wounded healer: Countertransference from a Jungian perspective*. London: Routledge.

Shuttleworth, J. (2012). Infant observation, ethnography and social anthropology. In C. Urwin & J. Sternberg (Eds.), *Infant observation and research: Emotional processes in everyday lives* (pp. 55–67). Hove and New York: Routledge.

Sills, C., & Salters, D. (1991). The comparative script system. *ITA News, 31*, 1–15.

Skovholt, T., & Trotter-Mathison, M. (2011). *The resilient practitioner: Counselling and psychotherapy. Investigating practice from scientific, historical and cultural perspectives*. New York and London: Routledge.

Smith, F. (1985). *Writing and the write*. London: Heinemann Educational Books.

Smith, J. (2015). *Qualitative psychology. A practical guide to research methods*. London: SAGE.

Smith, M. L., & Glass, G. V. (1977). Meta-analysis of psychotherapy outcome studies. *American Psychologist, 32*(9), 752–760.

Smith, M. L., Glass, G. V., & Miller, T. I. (1980). *The benefits of psychotherapy*. Baltimore MD: Johns Hopkins University Press.

Sousa, D. (2007). From Monet's paintings to Margaret's ducks: Divagations on phenomenological research. *Existential Analysis, 19*(1), 143–155.

Speedy, J. (2015). *Staring at the park: A poetic autoethnographic inquiry*. Walnut Creek, CA: Left Coast Press.

Spitzer, R. L., Kroenke, R., Williams, J. B., & Lowe, B. (2006). A brief measure for assessing generalized anxiety disorder: The GAD-7. *Archives of Internal Medicine, 166*, 1092–1097.

Spry, T. (2001). Performing autoethnography: An embodied methodological praxis. *Qualitative Inquiry, 7*(6), 706–732.

Stern, D. N. (2004). *The present moment in psychotherapy and everyday life*. New York: Norton Press.

Stiles, B. (2015). Theory building, enriching, and fact gathering: Alternative purposes of psychotherapy research. In Gelo (Ed.), *Psychotherapy research* (pp. 159–179). Wien: Springer-Verlag.

Stiles, W. B. (2007). Theory-building case studies of counselling and psychotherapy. *Counselling and Psychotherapy Research, 7*(2), 122–127.

Stiles, W. B., Barkham, M., Mellor-Clark, J., & Connell, J. (2008). Effectiveness of cognitive-behavioural, person-centred, and psychodynamic therapies in UK. Primary-care routine practice: Replication in a larger sample. *Psychological Medicine, 38*, 677–688.

Stiles, W. B., Barkham, M., Twigg, E., Mellor-Clark, J., & Cooper, M. (2006). Effectiveness of cognitive-behavioural, person-centred and psychodynamic therapies as practised in UK National Health Service settings. *Psychological Medicine, 36*, 555–566.

Sui, D. Z., & DeLyser, D. (2012). Crossing the qualitative-quantitative chasm I: Hybrid geographies, the spatial turn, and volunteered geographic information (VGI). *Progress in Human Geography, 36*(1), 111–124.

Sussman, M. B. (1992). *A curious calling: Unconscious motivations for practicing psychotherapy*. Lanham, MD: Jason Aronson.

Symington, N. (1986). *The analytic experience: Lectures from the Tavistock*. London: Free Association Books.

Taylor, B. (2006). *Reflective practice: A guide for nurses and midwives*. Maidenhead: Open University Press.

Thompson, K., & Adams, K. (Eds.). (2015). *Expressive writing: Counseling and healthcare*. London: Rowman & Littlefield.

Todres, L. (2007). *Embodied enquiry. Phenomenological touchstones for research, psychotherapy and spirituality*. London: Palgrave Macmillan.

Tracey, T. J., & Kokotovic, A. M. (1989). Factor structure of the Working Alliance Inventory. *Psychological Assessment: A Journal of Consulting and Clinical Psychology, 1*(3), 207–210.

Tullis, J. A. (2013). Self and others: Ethics in autoethnographic research. In S. Holman Jones, T. E. Adams, & C. Ellis (Eds.), *Handbook of autoethnography* (pp. 244–261). Walnut Creek, CA: Left Coast Press.

Urwin, C., & Sternberg, J. (Eds.) (2012). *Infant observation and research: Emotional processes in everyday lives* (pp. 55–67). Hove and New York: Routledge.

Valerio, P. (2017). *Introduction to countertransference in therapeutic practice: A myriad of mirrors*. London: Routledge.

Van Manen, M. (2017). Phenomenology in its original sense. *Qualitative Health Research, 27*(6), 810–825.

Varma, V. (Ed.). (1997). *The needs of counsellors and psychotherapists: Emotional, social, physical, professional*. London: SAGE.

Walfish, S., McAlister, B., O'Donnell, P., & Lambert, M. J. (2012). An investigation of self-assessment bias in mental health providers. *Psychological Reports, 110*(2), 639–644.

Wampold, B. (2001). *The great psychotherapy debate*. Mahwah, NJ: Lawrence Erlbaum Associates.

Wampold, B. E., & Imel, Z. E. (2015). *The great psychotherapy debate: The evidence for what makes psychotherapy work* (2nd ed.). New York: Routledge/Taylor & Francis.

White, S., Fook, J., & Gardner, F. (2008). *Critical reflection in health and social care*. Maidenhead: Open University Press.

Willig, C. (2012). *Qualitative interpretation and analysis in psychology*. Maidenhead: OU Press.

Willis, P. (1999). Looking for what it's really like: Phenomenology in reflective practice. *Studies in Continuing Education, 21*(1), 91–112. doi.org/10.1080/0158037990210106

Williamson, C., & Wright, J. K. (2018). How creative does writing have to be in order to be therapeutic? A dialogue on the practice and research of writing to recover and survive. *Journal of Poetry Therapy, 31*(2), 113–123.

Wright, H. (2009). Using an 'emergent design' to study adult education. *Educate,* Special Issue, 62–73. Retrieved from www.educatejournal.org/62.

Wright, J. K. (2003). Writing for protection: Reflective practice as a counsellor. *Journal of Poetry Therapy, 16*(4), 191–198.

Wright, J. K. (2009). Autoethnography and therapy writing on the move. *Qualitative Inquiry, 15*(4), 623–640.

Wright, J. K. (2012). Write, read, share, reflect. *Therapy Today, 23*(9), 22–25.

Wright, J. K. (2018). *Reflective writing in counselling and psychotherapy*. London: SAGE.

Wyatt, J., & Adams, T. E. (Eds.). (2014). *On (writing). families: Autoethnographies of presence and absence, love and loss*. Rotterdam: Sense.

Yalom, I. (1980). *Existential psychotherapy*. New York: Basic Books.

# Index

www.ingramcontent.com/pod-product-compliance
Lightning Source LLC
Chambersburg PA
CBHW080557030426
42336CB00019B/3225